RESET

THE END OF NEW ZEALAND'S NEOLIBERAL EXPERIMENT

JOHN MORGAN

SEABOURNE PUBLISHING

Published by Seabourne Publishing

Contact: seabourne.publishing@gmail.com

A catalogue record for this book is available from the National Library of New Zealand.

Cover design by Gary Cannell

CONTENTS

CHAPTER 1

YEAH-NAH!

Some people feel the rain. Others just get wet.

— Bob Marley

YEAH AND *NAH*, the colloquial words for *yes* and *no*, together, form that distinctively Kiwi contradictory idiom, *yeah-nah*. On the face of it *yeah-nah* is a throw-away, nonchalant statement of indifference, indecisiveness and complacency – verbal shorthand when one doesn't want to commit opinion – indeed, encapsulating our national psyche and the inherent lackadaisical nature of New Zealanders brought to our attention by author, social historian and raconteur Gordon McLauchlan in his portraits of a passionless people.

Yet it is more than just *not giving a shit* or a lack of enthusiasm. It is a uniquely informal Kiwi expression and socially acceptable way to say no, used in conversation when one has half an understanding of what another is saying, or when one doesn't fully agree – yet, you want to be included and want to know more. It expresses measures of trepidation and shyness: trepidation of feeling out of one's depth and shyness about standing out – being found and being seen. The subtlety of the slow, drawn out emphases on the *yeah* or the *nah*, is indication of the measure of agreement or disagreement – and the measure of desire to be included. In this sense, even if introverted, it is a measure of sincerity.

New Zealanders do enjoy an international reputation for being sincere, even if somewhat naïve. Too, we are renowned for being convivial, open and friendly with an informality and ease absent in Europe (while traditional Māori institutional protocols adhere to formal ritual, European colonists largely left theirs behind). We value traditional open-house hospitality that doesn't stand on ceremony and our penchant for backyard barbecues takes its cue from an outdoor heritage. A predominate characteristic we like to live by is our love of the land. Our desire to be outdoors in our own backyard and in the wider natural environment is overarching, and quite distinct from other nationalities. Australians, by contrast, see the outdoors as a hazardous place. And wisely so. It is.

Part-and-parcel of the value we place on an outdoor heritage is that we like to consider ourselves to be resourceful, independent – a DIY pragmatic people, forged, merged and morphed from the intrepidness of daring Polynesians and restless, enterprising British migrants. Indeed, we have enjoyed a reputation for being an adventurous, pragmatic figure-it-out-and-fix-it-up people whose ideas have been a prime export commodity, prompting Robert Muldoon, when Prime Minister and challenged about the increasing numbers of people leaving to work in Australia, to respond, *it raised the IQ of both nations.*

It has to be said, though, the *number-eight-wire* mythology is wearing a little tiresome. Contrary to being uniquely Kiwi, the cherished self-portrait of the reliant, adaptable, country man of the backblocks was common to all pioneering societies. For sure it may have lasted longer in New Zealand, into the 1980s, with families maintaining 'quarter-acre block' homes and a thirty- to forty-year-old car fleet. But most people today have neither the time nor inclination to spend in that way. And the rugby-hardened peasant farmers of yore have largely morphed into digital savvy, corporate landowners and functionaries of commerce.

As well, we like to think of ourselves as being, in the main, an honest people – an attribute lived, respected, and expected of others. With a live-and-let-live outlook and strong sense of fairness, we are equally wary of groups who think they are entitled to bully others, and groups who think they are entitled to special protection against criticism. Having a can-do attitude, we expect everyone to pull their weight and no recompense is expected beyond a fair day's pay for a fair day's work – lending to our history as a non-tipping culture. A culture of honesty, fairness, doing for yourself and not expecting others to do for you, and non-gratuity, provide the foundations for New Zealand being credited as the top-most least corrupt nation in the world[1] – a position we have shared jointly with Denmark in recent years. Too, the fact that we are such a small population, that in conversation with a stranger one can establish that you know someone who knows someone, who knows someone, the other person knows. Such intimacy, overlapping networks and commonality make it difficult to pursue underhand activities and keep below the radar.

There was a time when such attitudes of fairness, intimacy and connectedness were a contributing factor to New Zealand's reputation as a largely egalitarian community – a tradition for which, at one time, Kiwis were proud. It was an era when we recognised that it was our social and economic interdependence which made our personal independence possible. We invested in collective well-being which gave individuals the freedom and security to do what they wanted, to pursue fulfilling lives.

Sadly, those are long bygone days. Our egalitarian and coherent community is long a thing of the past. The impact of thirty-five years of neoliberal monetarist orthodoxy on New Zealand's egalitarian society has been profoundly adverse. Neoliberalism is characterised by market fundamentalism – a shift away from social provision to individualised responsibility, deregulated labour, deregulated trade and unfettered financial markets – which monetarism greatly assists. Monetarism is characterised by independent central banks having free license to manage the economy through control of interest rates and the money supply, abetted by hands off government. And restrictions on banks to lend for productive purposes alone were lifted, enabling them to speculate on the open market for their own profit-making. Emphasis has been placed on short-term profit over long-term prudence. It has resulted in New Zealand being ranked today amongst the most unequal of countries in the developed world, living with high rates of social dysfunction, less trust and social mobility between people – cancerous problems that have been let to persist with loss of societal coherence.

The pursuit of an economic philosophy promoting individual selfishness and group self-interestedness has chipped away at shared community, our sense of identity and shared destiny. Disparities of income and security have created the prevailing disparities between *have-yachts* and *have-nots*. Ironically, the *have-yachts* and the *have-nots* have one thing in common – a self-righteous sense of entitlement. The *have-yachts* believe their wealth to be justly earned and deserved, and expect their privileges to be protected to the disadvantage of others. The *have-nots*, whose plight is largely unjust and not of their making, expect their disadvantage to be unquestioningly compensated by the State, and feel justified to scam when the offerings are meagre and not served up as morning tea in bed.

I am of a family of first generation white New Zealanders. My parents and two older brothers, post-World War II immigrants born of an economically exhausted and war-weary Britain. My father was ex-Royal Navy and fell in love with New Zealand in the mid-1930s before the war, when stationed at Devonport Naval Base, Auckland, for two years. He left New Zealand promising to return.

To the fraternity of Pākehā Kiwis, my parents were *pommy* immigrants. Notwithstanding the fact my father was Welsh, no one could pin the 1960s–70s derogatory label of *whinging pom* to him. He sometimes reminisced with fellow British Islanders, but never bemoaned life in New Zealand. On the contrary, father would spread butter thickly on his bread, bite into it, savour the bite and, looking satisfyingly at the slice in his hand, would say, *I like to see my teeth marks in the butte*r. Literally living off the fat of the land, he loved it.

Should my father return from the grave and I were to ask him if New Zealand was still the epitome of the utopian state he had found and relished, and if he were to respond in the *lingua franca* of the day, I have no doubt his response would be a drawn out, demurring, *yeah-nah*, with long but equal emphasis on each word. Gone is the honest and decent nation my immigrant father found and relished. Gone is the sense of well-being, shared destiny, camaraderie and trust.

I strongly identify with New Zealand landscape and with being Pākehā and cannot live for an indefinite period of time in another country without refreshing my New Zealand identity. Each time I fill in an immigration entry card I love to write my *nationality as shown on passport* to be 'New Zealander'. And love to write 'New Zealand' in response to the question *what country were you born in?* I feel blessed, and know I am blessed. But, I do not take pride in what New

Zealand has become. The thirty-year-plus-blinkered-pursuit of neoliberalism has encouraged the turning of blind eyes to pervasive societal and environmental dysfunctions. Inadvertently, the Covid-19 pandemic has turned up the lighting on many of these matters, no longer able to be ignored by those who have preferred to do so – shortcomings in provision for health, education, housing, infrastructure, security of income, environmental standards.

I have long hankered for the day when the general consensus will again agree there are bigger equations involved in how we manage our economic affairs, other than our current simple and single-minded focus on micro-operational profit and loss. The slow response to the contrary, I believe, is due to the fact that neoliberalism is no longer *neo*. Men and women in their forties and prime of life have known no other way by which the world can be managed. Yet, all is not lost – nor beyond repair. Our sense of Kiwi-fairness, and our love of the land and outdoor heritage, may belatedly be gathering a momentum of discomfort with the normalising of social and economic dysfunctions, and anxiety about chronic and corrosive damage to the natural environment. Concern that New Zealand has run adrift and been floundering has given rise to a belated recognition of the need for greater ambition in the political realm to face inconvenient truths – an acknowledgement we live in a depleted and despondent country and that hands-on governance and management is required to do something about it.

Providence has dealt a moment of reflection – Covid-19's impact a time to take pause – to take stock of the pathway we are on. Government has been given licence to spend large in effort to mitigate the debilitating impact of the pandemic – to keep people solvent and stimulate the economy. It is an embrace of the interventionist doctrines of Keynesian macroeconomic practice that pulled nations through the Great Depression, World War II and the post-war 1945–73 economic expansion when governments chose policies that gave way to our most equal times and the great prosperity of the 1960s–70s. Unfortunately, the prompt for our embrace of Keynesian practice has come too late and caught us on the back foot out of balance, as opposed to deliberated forward steps to fund asserted transformative change. Nevertheless, we have been gifted a once in a lifetime opportunity to reimagine a new Aotearoa/New Zealand. The strong mandate delivered by the 2020 electoral outcome has empowered government agency to break from the status quo – opportunity to assert progressive transformative change – to reconfigure for a resilient, futuristic economy.

The ensuing dissertation likens neoliberalism and its hand-in-glove monetarist economic orthodoxy to the surrealism of Alice in Wonderland. It argues in favour of a 21st-century political realignment with our historical social–democratic predispositions. Prior to regaling you on the mechanics and effects of modern-day neoliberalism, I first overview what it is that makes us Kiwi. It is a sweep over New Zealand's natural, social and economic history from Gondwana to recent-year current affairs. I reflect on our uniqueness and quirkiness, sitting as we do on our few little rocks sticking out of the South Pacific Ocean. I reflect on our identity and values, doubts about our history, tentativeness about our future.

We are geologically young yet host to the most ancient forests on the planet supporting a unique and distinctive bird and insect fauna. Not only is Aotearoa/New Zealand a young country in its geology but also its history of human settlement. It was the last substantial landmass on Earth to be colonised by people and is the newest economy in the world. Yet we are one of the world's oldest and most stable democracies. We, the peoples of the newest economy and most stable of democracies, have forged a well-educated, well-ordered, multi-racial, democratic country, free of religious restrictions and indoctrinations. We have developed a technologically advanced nation with effective civil institutions and physical infrastructure, and the most efficient agricultural production in the world. We are recognised and acknowledged internationally for a history of being innovators of social change, acting collaboratively and constructively on the world stage, as well as being global achievers in activities ranging from sport and agriculture to science.

It rains a lot in New Zealand – perhaps opportune to splash in the puddles and feel the rain on our faces, to connect with our heartfelt selves, laugh and share with others. Unrestricted by history and tradition, we are a young, flexible, adaptable nation. We are perceived to be a kind people from a good country. It is beholden on us each to reconnect with our 'foundational native selves' and reshape a society about which we can boast when gathered around the barbecue, *modestly, of course*. And be thankful to be alive in a country as fortunate as ours.

CHAPTER 2

LAND OF TWO HALVES

We are a diverse and divided little country, uncertain of our future, doubtful about our past.

— IAN CROSS

New Boy Demeanour

ABOUT 250 MILLION YEARS AGO, the piece of the Earth's crust that is recognised today as New Zealand was sedimentary material lying subsurface on the edge of the vast giant supercontinent of Gondwana. Tectonic earth movements began to move the materials, and about 80 million years ago a marginal chunk separated to form ancestral *Zealandia*. A mini-continent half the size of Australia, *Zealandia* extends as far north as New Caledonia and south to Campbell and Auckland Islands. Gondwana was to further fragment with the spawning of Antarctica and Australia.

Zealandia the continent has bobbed up-and-down in our remote corner of the South Pacific Ocean, a reshaping archipelago of islands never fully submerged, as if ducking to hide but keeping an eye on the passage of time. Only 7 percent of ancestral *Zealandia* sits above sea level today, and still peeking are the emergent islands we have come to know as Aotearoa/New Zealand, the sunken remnant of *Zealandia* existing as our continental shelf.

Out of the cracks of the vastness of geological time, about 150,000 years ago, a naked ape, standing on two legs, walked out of Africa. Akin to a plague of insects, *Homo sapiens* sprawled over continental Europe and Asia, sidled into Canada, and spread down the Americas. When doing so they superseded and overwhelmed other human species and exterminated and devastated existing wildlife – literally butchering their way, leaving in their wake ecosystems transformed beyond recognition. *Homo sapiens* arrived in Australia about 45,000 years ago. Perhaps observing from a distance, wary and a little shy, New Zealand endeavoured to keep out of the fray of all the goings-on. And successfully keep out of the fray it did, for it was only about 800 years ago when the inevitable happened and humans beached themselves on its shores.

Geographically challenged Americans might think that you get to New Zealand by driving over the Sydney harbour bridge. While Australia and New Zealand do have closely related British colonial histories, our respective natural and social histories are like chalk and cheese – which lend to different temperaments of our peoples, and different cultural, societal and political values.

Australia, an eroded and scalped fragment of Gondwana, is as ancient as any landmass on Earth. New Zealand, originating of sedimentary materials, is a geological newborn baby. Australian natural heritage has been tempered and tested by fire. New Zealand's has been moulded and blessed by water. Australia's expansive desert environs starkly contrast that of New Zealand's, at one time, clad chest to shin in dense, temperate, wet forests. Biological survival in the harshness of Australian climate and conditions evolved forms of plant and animal life, nearly all of which are designed to *get you* in some way or another. New Zealand was bereft of large terrestrial mammals, and the wet, lush temperate forests nurtured fleshy flora, and a fauna population of shy ground-dwelling birds.

Fire and water today are our respective land management issues. These earthly elements indicative of the temperaments of our national psyches – Australia, a land of ornery, get-out-of-my-face wheelers and dealers; we, an island of consensual living, laissez-faire pleasure seekers, always looking to go to the local creek or the beach to fish or swim. I think it insightful that New Zealanders characterise themselves as Kiwis. Australian birdlife is in your face – prolific, raucous, colourful and brash. The ground-dwelling nocturnal kiwi is dowdy coloured, shy and retiring, albeit endearing with its awkward and humorous running style.

Australia's landscape is home to the oldest living human culture on Earth. New Zealand is host to the youngest human culture on Earth. Established as a prison colony, Australian colonials were embittered convicts torn from their homelands, forced to get on with being Australian. New Zealand's colonials chose, for whatever reasons, to be here, albeit reminiscing for a culture left behind. While Australian Aboriginal and European cultures remain distinctly separate, Māori and Pākehā cultures are, not so unperceptively, morphing into a distinctive New Zealand identity. Compared with nations worldwide that share colonial histories, and their socio-political relationships with their first-nation-peoples, New Zealand is very much at the forefront of establishing political, and dare I say, congenial and familial bicultural relations with every cause for optimism.

New Zealand is new in the fullest sense – geologically, biologically and socially. Being the last landmass on Earth to be discovered and settled by people, it is by every account, the new boy on the street of nations. There has been tentativeness in the history of our new boy demeanour, a predisposition to not believe we were any good at anything unless people overseas told us we were so. We have not been a nation of people that have sought to create symbols of our distinctiveness. Māori didn't give the country a name – Aotearoa was concocted, with strong European input, in the latter part of the 19th century. The Dutch name *Nieuw Zeeland* was given by Joan Blaeu, a cartographer for the Dutch East India Company, sitting at his workstation in Amsterdam. Our Head of State is a woman called Windsor, living in the world's oldest inhabited castle in London. Our flag is barely distinguishable from that of our closest neighbour.

But we do seem to have an innate consciousness of a modest identity different from that of others even if we have difficulty articulating it. A hundred and twenty years ago we had the insightfulness to realise we were different from our cousins across the water. When it was first mooted in 1890 to federate with them, our response was an equivocal *yeah-nah*. In 1901, the emphasis was an unequivocal long drawn out *nah* and we formalised our choice not to become Australia's seventh state.

Unusual as it is, our history of gaining sovereignty has parallel to no other nation. Our constitutional status and independence from Britain evolved incrementally and at times, on our part, reluctantly. The advent of independence remains the subject of academic debate and we have no day on which it is commemorated. Admittedly, this circumstance was driven as much as anything by an attitude we were *more British than the British* and the notion of not being directly united with Empire, and constitutionally attached to the British Crown, was incomprehensible.

The 1931 Statute of Westminster enabled us to become as independent as we wished yet it was fully fifty-five years later, when the Lange Labour Government passed the Constitution Act 1986, before New Zealand chose to take on full legal independence. To be sure, the Statute of Westminster was adopted sixteen years later in 1947, at which time New Zealand citizenship came into existence. But legally and emotionally we remained ambivalent. Indeed, we maintained two national anthems into the 1970s, *God Save the Queen* being of primary importance and *God Defend New Zealand* of secondary importance. Any baby-boomer will tell you they were ignorant of the lyrics to *God Defend New Zealand*, yet when at the movies, stood for the national anthem of *God Save the Queen* before the film began. And in 2021 the British Monarch still graces all our coinage and $20 notes.

No doubt, our growing-up pains have been compounded by the fact that we have been sparsely and lowly populated and lacked the confidence to go it alone. In the whole of recorded history, there have only been about 15 million New Zealanders. Mistakes have been made and continue to be made by that tiny number but New Zealand is doing as well as any flummoxed first-time parent.

Geological History with a Twist

It was the joint effort of the Antarctic, Indian and Pacific tectonic plates, 80–60 million years ago, that led to the fragmentation of Gondwana and the current positional placement of New Zealand, sitting as it does, precariously on the outer south-western edge of the Indian plate where it is at loggerheads with the Pacific Plate.

The North Island rides the Indian Plate (the Pacific Plate sub-ducting) and the South Island rides the Pacific Plate (the Indian Plate sub-ducting). Caught in the middle and straddling this splitting, scissor-opening contortion, New Zealand is being twisted and torn apart. The eastern side of the country is shearing southwards relative to the west, splitting the country in two, sliding hundreds of kilometres south, giving rise to the mountain chains buckling upwards along the Alpine Fault. These awesome forces vex us, as in the wake of the 2011 Christchurch and 2016 Kaikoura earthquake events, we grapple with the rather quaint notion of retrofitting old buildings and constructing the new to withstand them.

In contrast to the south being speared by subterranean rock formations, the face of the north is being pock-marked by sulphurous extrusions. The volcanic activity is the result of a double whammy. Not only is there the typical occurrence of sub-ducted (Pacific) crustal materials melting and squirting back up to the surface through the faults of the overlying (Indian) crust, but a clockwise rotation of the North Island twisting about its centre has been tearing, stretching and thinning the North Island crust, creating the volcanic rift we witness today. About 20 million years ago East Cape probably lay alongside Northland; sliding southwards it left behind a migrating belt of volcanic activity in its wake – 15 million years ago Great Barrier was in eruption, 10 million years ago Coromandel peninsula, and the current day volcanic zone in which volcanoes started to rise, about 2 million years ago. The stretching and thinning of the Earth's crust that has formed the North Island volcanic zone has torn the geological equivalent of an open, festering wound. Within its 240km by 50km boundaries have occurred some of the most violent volcanic eruptions the world has known.

The Pacific Plate in the south thrusting up, the Pacific Plate in the north diving down, the spinal column twisting, body parts stretching: the fish of Maui threshing and writhing on the water's surface and the waka from which it has been caught rising on its wake. How did archaic Māori know that Hawke's Bay looks like a fish hook? No GPS to be had! How did they know the North Island looks like a threshing fish plunging into the water's surface? How did they know the South Island looked like a waka, rising as it is on a wave of energy manifest as rock?

Māori mythology informs us Maui was no ordinary person. A somewhat mischievous demigod, he applied his courage and daring to do a few good deeds. His fishing up of the North Island was to pique his older brothers and prove his worthiness to go out fishing with them. It's his brothers we have to thank for the rugged topography of New Zealand landscape. While Maui set out to rally the troops to help deal with the monstrous fish he had brought to the surface, his brothers tired of his absence, and began to randomly carve up the catch for themselves. Their greedy, frenetic chopping mutilated the body of the fish forming the mountains, gullies and the rugged topography over and around which, today, New Zealanders have to manoeuvre.

Lending to somewhat dangerous New Zealand driving traits. Historically populated by widely dispersed small rural communities and individual families in remote, isolated locations, New Zealanders learnt to drive on narrow roads carrying little traffic, and I believe, have become genetically programmed to *on-farm* driving. Most are very reluctant users of indicators, *can't they see which way I am turning?*, and habitually cut corners – mindless habits ingrained by not having need to see beyond one's nose, *mind you some of us have very big noses*. And I have yet to determine which is more stupid – driving over the centre line on a blind corner, or directly in front of observed on-coming traffic. Providing grist for those who argue a need to have road median barriers installed nationwide to protect ourselves from ourselves. And as for round-a-bouts! For some reason, the circle in the middle of the road totally short-circuits the *on-farm* driving programme and all variations of signalling behaviour can be observed. Evolutionary fitness has yet to determine who wins here and there could well evolve a unique driving species, endemic to New Zealand.

Natural History in the Nude

Endemism is a term to describe organisms restricted to one place and found nowhere else. The level of endemism attained in our plants and animals is among the highest in the world, and New Zealand ranks with the islands of Hawaii and Galapagos. Ancestral *Zealandia*, physically isolated from the rest of the world by oceans of water for the 65 million years dinosaurs have been extinct, enabled evolutionary pathways that were not possible anywhere else. Plants and animals evolved independent of the environmental circumstances that prevailed on other parts of Earth. However, shy primordial New Zealand was unable to keep out of the evolutionary fray forever. Polynesians arrived and established some 800 years ago. Consistent with the arrival of the naked ape to every other part of the world, New Zealand nature suffered the arrival of *Homo sapiens*. Landscape was denuded of its vegetation, and wildlife severely pressured both by hunting and loss of habitat. Māori hunted eleven species of moa to extinction, and with their prey gone, so too did the giant Eyles's harrier and the largest eagle known on Earth, the giant Haast eagle, disappear. By the time of Captain James Cook's first landings, half of New Zealand's birds were already extinct. Birds that survived, survived in remoteness.

Europeans began to establish a little over 200 years ago, after which New Zealand suffered the most rapid rate of forest clearance and habitat modification of any nation on Earth. Changes to landscape that happened over two millennia in Europe happened within 100 years in New Zealand, particularly the 50-year period from 1850 to

1900. It is obvious why kauri were prized – they are amongst the largest trees in the world, holding the record for the greatest timber volume of any one tree. Pushed to the verge of extinction, the total area of kauri today is less than 3 percent of its original extent. But also, kahikatea forests were burnt off for the wetlands on which they grew to be drained and developed into pasture. Regions of wild landscape remain today not through insightful forethought and protection but because their rugged remoteness helped protect them from the severity of the ravaging of people. Today, threats once posed to our remnant archaic forests by fire, axe then bulldozer have been replaced with those posed by plant pathogens. The risks aggravated by the warming effects of climate change.

Coinciding with European acquisition of confiscated Māori lands after the wars of the 1860s, wholesale clearance of North Island forests and expansion of pastoral agriculture was fuelled by the expansion of the railways in the late 1800s, then the advent of refrigeration, enabling exports of meat and dairy produce. A new landscape emerged – that of the widespread grassland system for which New Zealand is internationally renowned. By the mid-1970s the sheep population stood at about 70 million, outnumbering people 25:1. In the mid-1980s it became evident that government subsidies, to encourage land clearance to graze even more sheep, were the cause of severe land erosion on marginal lands not suitable for grazing. The cessation of subsidies more than halved the sheep population to about 30 million over the past three decades.

But land erosion problems have morphed into water pollution problems. A two-decade long intensification of irrigation and stocking rates, aided and abetted by a central-government drive to double dairy exports, resulted in a massive shift in land-use from sheep farming to irrigated dairying. The dairy herd doubled, enabled by a five-fold increase in the use of nitrogen, leading to increased greenhouse gas emissions and degradation of fresh water quality. It's a simple correlation of more cows, more shit on the ground, more water use, more nitrogen run-off, more effluent run-off. Nutrients and pathogens entering waterways and water bodies are of such volume that those creeks we used to swim in are, today, not so swimmable.

As well as the denudation of landscape and recent year denigration of water quality, colonial New Zealand experienced rapid and significant change in the composition of its animal wildlife populations. European settlers, homesick and in attempt to create a home-away-from-home, introduced European plant and animal species. This history is, as we say, 'history' with little need to be relitigated here. Suffice to say that mammals arrived en force onto New Zealand and that the *Zealandia* of old would never be so again. It was a leap-frog over a threshold from which there was no coming back.

Denuded of vegetation, New Zealand native wildlife populations diminished in direct correlation to the scalping of their dense temperate forest habitats. Today New Zealand has the highest proportion of indigenous species in the world threatened with or at risk of extinction. Ministry for the Environment and StatsNZ reports *Our Land 2018* and *Environment Aotearoa* 2019 conferred that status to 90 percent of seabirds, 84 percent of reptiles, 76 percent of freshwater fish and 74 percent of terrestrial birds. The North Island brown kiwi – our endearing flightless bird which has become our iconic symbol of endemism – continues to decline at a rate of 2–3 percent every year. In the 21st century we are in need of empowered effort to nurture the nature that is a heartfelt component of our national identity.

Social History in the Stars

The Polynesian triangle between Hawaii, Easter Island and Aotearoa/New Zealand was the last region of Earth to be settled by people, expansion into the Pacific beginning about 3300 years ago. New Zealand was first settled by Polynesians from the Cook Islands and the Marquesas who started arriving sometime about 800 years ago with some evidence of a later infusion of arrivals from Tahiti. There was no mass migration as depicted by Charles F Goldie and Louis John Steele (1898) in their romanticised artwork 'The Arrival of the Maoris in New Zealand' – that of canoes laden with sprawling, weakened and starved people enlivened by the sight of *the land of the long white cloud* on the horizon. Rather, settlement occurred by the arrival of a few canoes at a time, over prolonged periods, now thought to be purposeful navigations to and from distant island homelands.

These people explored and navigated the vastness of the Pacific Ocean by ocean currents, winds and stars, and deserve a reputation as the Vikings of the South Pacific. Put into context, these sailors seemed to know where they were going long before the angst-ridden adventures of Magellan and Columbus. Research by University of Otago biological anthropologist, Lisa Matisoo-Smith, has shown that the ancestors of modern Polynesians had travelled to and been in Chile, almost a century before Columbus first arrived at America in 1492. Indeed, we are only just beginning to appreciate the important role Tahitian Tupaia played when he boarded the *Endeavour* to accompany Captain James Cook. Notwithstanding the fact he could understand the language of a people living on a remote southern ocean island 1800 kilometres south of his native island, Tupaia drew a chart centred on Ra'iatea encompassing a 4000-kilometre sweep of the Pacific Ocean. He was able to accurately predict where and when an island would appear on the horizon, recite given names and how long it would take to reach them.

It is at Wairau Bar, near modern-day Blenheim, where the evidence of the earliest Polynesian settlement seems to have been established in the early 1300s. Archaeological surveys began in 2009 and reports on their findings started to come to light in 2013. Excavations undertaken by University of Otago archaeologist Richard Walter have convinced him the Wairau Bar is the birth place of our nation, 'a large village site of a wealthy and successful community and probably the first major economic and ritual centre in the new colony'[1]. Hardly the remnants of some washed-up, blown-to-shore fishing trip gone wrong. Arguably those people came here on purpose, prepared to stay – they were of a people who had been making voyages on this scale for millennia. Having reached and settled the most inaccessible habitable land on Earth, their voyage has to be one of the last and greatest feats of celestial navigation and human settlement; the long journey of *sapiens* from East Africa's Rift Valley 150,000 years prior, ending here on the north-east of the South Island of New Zealand, in Marlborough, at the outlet of the Wairau River.

Pleiades and the Southern Cross parade in drilled and inexorable order across our night sky, apparently in an order so meticulous, that the precise pattern overhead is enough for those who have the skills, to read not just the season of the year but hour of night. There is no place on earth Pleiades cannot be seen. Comprising a group of seven stars, the constellation was mythologised by the Greeks as a cohort of sisters. Known to Māori as Matariki, the seven stars too were mythologised by Māori as women. As did Pleiades serve as a navigation beacon for European ocean-going voyagers, so did Matariki, *the eyes of God*, guide Polynesians over the expansive Pacific Ocean. In New Zealand, Matariki comes into view just before dawn, early June, and we enjoy a recent-year renaissance in midwinter ceremony acknowledging the rise of Matariki and the traditional Māori New Year.

More distinctive and ever-present in our night sky is the Southern Cross. Of significance to southern Pacific islands and Australia, it too has been important for other civilisations, including the Egyptians and the Incas. It is known by at least eight different names to Māori. Sixteenth-century European explorers saw it as an affirmation of their Christian faiths, hence the name the constellation is widely known by today. Its prominence in the South Pacific has lent to its importance on island nation ensigns asserting to other nation states our position in the southern ocean. It is one of the first star patterns that New Zealand children learn to recognise and 800 years after the arrival of the first people, it has become a symbol of New Zealand nationhood.

The New Zealand flag is barely distinguishable from that of our closest neighbour, Australia, both flying a bold portrayal of the Southern Cross imposed on a royal blue background accompanied by the Union Jack identifying our common colonial history with Imperial Britain. Many New Zealanders, if challenged, don't know the difference between the two flags. Long-standing social conversation about the need to address the confusing likeness culminated in the change-of-flag-referendum initiated in 2015. However, the process succumbed to popular dissent and the March 2016 vote clearly supported maintaining the status quo. Support for the status quo more an expression of cynicism about the process, politicised as it was by then Prime Minister John Key's agenda to commodify New Zealand as a silver fern.

In keeping with the persona of John Key, the flag debate revolved around the issue of cosmetics. More important, gutsy stuff needed to be dealt with beforehand – issues on the need or otherwise of having our own Head of State and a New Zealand constitution. The resolution of these matters would flow on naturally to a representative ensign. Given the excellence of artwork on our paper currency, I have every confidence that a design of suitable dignity could result.

The uniqueness of our social history is apparent in discussion on constitutional matters. Two principal cultures have held sway, today shared by communities of many diverse ethnicities. We are a recent year island state with a continuing history of immigration and settlement by different peoples. All the while, our domestic socio-political history developed strong predispositions for social democracy. It has not been all plain sailing – there have been moments of earth-shaking tremors and confused indication on tortuous roads.

CHAPTER 3

ANATOMY OF RESTLESSNESS

Experience is not what happens to a man. It is what a man does with what happens to him.

— Aldous Huxley

The post-World War II years leading up to the early 1970s were a period of conservative prosperity. I have a family photo taken early 1963 – it is a photo of its time. Captured is a secure yet unpretentious family, well fed, content and with an unassuming confidence: secure in the State house that came with the secure government job provided by a nation steeped in the ethos of welfare economics. Content, and humble even, in the knowledge that social democracy ensured a fair and equitable ability to live life in a nation priding itself in its egalitarian ethos. Maybe unaware, but comfortable, nevertheless, in a booming economy and a nation secure in its role as a dependable supplier of primary produce to powerful Western political and economic partners. It is a snapshot of very recent New Zealand history, which seems bygone before I have gone, and the values it represents, for which I continue to hanker.

My childhood innocence was indicative of New Zealand's social naïvety of the day. Being able to drink tank rainwater with squirming mosquito larvae; be away from home all day, dam and play in creeks; parents trusting other parents to be mindful of their children; leaving the car unlocked where you park to go shopping; and leaving the house unlocked when going away on holiday so the neighbours can get in.

When the good times began to fade in the 1980s, we started to lock our car doors and our homes. Things were looser in the 1960s and 70s. Then they grew ugly. Dope growing was fun, then it became razor wire, dogs and gangs. Music was about good times, then it was about *mother-fuckers* and *gangsta-gunnings*. It was a time when police had a face one could relate to. They were, as is necessary, authoritative agents, yet were in the main fair-dealing functionaries of the extended community. These were days when a murder was so rare it was nationwide news. Today they seem to occur every weekend. Who can blame the police for becoming hardened and faceless with a 'gang culture' of their own?

There is a sense of deterioration in our social environment, which is often blamed on a moral decline. This may well be, but it is as much inherent economic injustice. At the core of my lament is the loss of egalitarian values, in which at one time the whole nation took pride. There has always been and always will be those better off than others. That is not the issue. The issue is the gap between those with much more than enough and the increasing number of those with much less than enough.

Cultural Revolution with a Twist

Rural life on the farm 1950s-60s was still a part of urban consciousness. We were secure and egalitarian, up to a point. While

Māori lived poorly, we boasted a happy co-existence. They appeared happy with their lot, working in the shearing sheds or living on the edge of town and working in the freezing works. Society was friendly and cohesive. We chatted with the neighbours over the back fence but there was always a gap in the hedge through which they could gain access. It was a deeply conservative era – but for good reasons. That generation's attitudes had been inculcated by the experience of growing up in the poverty of the Great Depression and returning from the trauma of warfare. Hardly surprising they aspired to the stable, secure, quiet and comfortable – left alone to get on with the ordinary, unexciting humdrum of everyday life.

For the up-coming younger generation, experience of life lived in the post-war years seemed drab, joyless, conformist, stifling. The comfort and security enjoyed nurtured hunger for excitement and passion, giving rise to parental-generation angst about an American-influenced teenage subculture, morally delinquent and promiscuous. For sure enough, it was the coming-out of a restless generation in a repressive social environment – precursor symptoms for the unstoppable social change that began to emancipate New Zealand from its conformist culture.

By the end of the 1960s, jet airliners enabled accessible international travel, once the preserve of the wealthy. Too, we had television in our living rooms, enabling us to eavesdrop on the world. Mass communication of news and ideas with the rest of the world, in a way never before had, was foment for a massive sociological shift – a state of societal and political flux was to ensue. It was a momentous decade that came with quantum leaps in attitudes, music, fashion and lifestyles. Women joined the workforce, divorce lost its social stigma and alternative living arrangements were to be seen – mixed flatting, de-facto relationships and solo parenthood. Hippie culture, women's protest, Māori protest, flourished. Civil rights movements in the US made their presence felt, all the while the Vietnam War raged and anti-war movements prevailed. And environmentalism was given impetus by Rachael Carson's book *Silent Spring*.

New Zealand's no-nuclear stance was born in the 1960s. Protestors were saying no to US nuclear frigates and submarines and our politicians were taking the French to task over their continued nuclear testing in the Pacific. It was the dawn of a wider public environmental consciousness and green politics. Anti-Vietnam War rallies and environmental concerns gave birth to the Values Party and the Green Party. We were (and still are) a culture a long way from being imbued in a Mediterranean ambience of 'wine, women and song' but the mantra of 'rugby, racing and beer' was being diluted.

The 1970s kicked off with student activist Tim Shadbolt being jailed for three months for saying *bullshit* in public. But 1970s New Zealand is a decade that belongs to Māori protest and its achievements. It was the groundswell that has led us to this day, and days yet to come, of Māori articulating, ever more powerfully, issues of historical grievance and asserting 21st-century bicultural rights.

At the end of the Second World War, Māori counted about 100,000. By the end of the century there were 600,000. As Māori grew in numbers and confidence, they began to claim a bigger share of power and wealth. Formidable Ngā Puhi kuia, Whina Cooper, led her famous 1975 land march from Te Hāpua in the Far North to the footsteps of Parliament. She set out with her mokopuna and the call to march *not one acre more*. They arrived in Wellington in their thousands. Auckland iwi Ngāti Whātua defied government for five years culminating in the occupation of Bastion Point to prevent transfer of their lands to private ownership for residential development. Eva Rickard took her stand at Raglan Golf Course over the alienation of her iwi's land. In both instances, land taken ostensibly for military purposes during wartime was given to local authorities at war's end.

A history of land loss had continued throughout the 1900s, different in degree to the confiscations of the mid-1800s, but protracted, stealthy attrition, nevertheless. Protest and demands made to honour the Treaty of Waitangi were so successful that Treaty provisions were built into new law. The Waitangi Tribunal was established in 1975 and ten years later given stronger powers. Out of the 1981 Springbok tour protest came an uneasy soul search about racism on home turf, the debate giving stimulus to the emergent Māori renaissance. Newly appointed Assistant Māori Commissioner for Children, Glenis Philip-Barbara, made the somewhat poignant statement, she grew up feeling unwelcome in her own country[1].

Land grievances and Treaty rights remain central to Māori politics. Lands, forests and money began to be handed over by the State. Growing political strength was shown in election outcomes and, at the turn of the century, the formation of Māori political parties. Indeed, it was the foreshore and seabed conundrum that crystallised the formation of the Māori Party in 2005. The Clark-Cullen Labour Government, which presided for three terms of government, was brought to heel by the splintering of its Māori members. The fragmentation of Labour saw its demise to the incoming Key-English National Government 2008 in coalition with the new Māori Party. I felt the hurt of the Māori Party when the onrush of the 2017 Ardern-Robertson election campaign bled its support base. And took heart from their impressive resurgence in the 2020 election.

We have arrived at the debate on how our unique socio-political circumstances could be encapsulated in constitutional form. We have world-leading legislation whereby the Whanganui River and Te Urewera are legal entities in their own right – recognised and understood as living and legal persons. What was known as Te Urewera National Park is now overseen and managed as a separate territory by Tūhoe, the people of Te Urewera, in partnership with the Department of Conservation. Are we able to include the Māori view of tino rangatiratanga (autonomy) and their traditional models of leadership, with the governorship of a unitary state? There has always been tension in Māori politics, between desire to manage their own affairs and an inconvenient arranged marriage with democracy. Having no choice but to make the Westminster model of governance work for them, a preferential alignment with Labour Party values seemed to prevail. Yet that alignment sat awkwardly with scepticism of the State. The dichotomy no better illustrated than the Ratana Party linking itself with Labour and holding the four Māori seats for fifty years. And Donna Awatere, Member of Parliament for ACT, epitomising individualism – personal responsibility and self-reliance.

Early 1960s I attended a very small rural primary school with a high proportion of Māori children. Nearly everyone could play a ukulele and/or guitar. For those who didn't, the fundamental skills were soon imparted. The shelter shed on the school playground was often the location of an impromptu concert initiated by an individual but often followed up by others when the instrument was passed around. Within days of particular songs hitting the charts I would hear them live, as was the case when the dance phenomenon the Twist hit New Zealand, 1961, and I was listening to renditions of Chubby Checker's songs *The Twist* and *Let's Twist Again* in our school shelter shed.

The Twist dance phenomenon was the beginning of partners dancing separately. This led to the contemporary practice of individuals *boogying* on the dance floor in loose association with others, and my generation was the first to lose the social skills to dance in unison with another – considered a fundamental social skill by generations past. With the benefit of hindsight, it was a portent for a new world of 'individualism' just under the horizon – a world of the distinct rights and needs of the individual over and above collective community.

The arrival of the 2017 Ardern-Robertson coalition with NZ First fifty-six years later was enabled by a growing discomfort and reawakening desire to reconsider our parting of the ways from collectivism. The coalition put into action a demonstrable shift from laissez-faire governance, getting their hands dirty addressing social, economic and environmental malfunctions. Yet strong elements of reticence remain evident and gutsy transformative change eluded us.

The resounding mandate given by the 2020 election to the Labour and Green cohort of ministers was largely promoted by integrity of leadership in the face of multiple crises (particularly fear of Covid-19) and delivered by National Party disarray. While desire for realignment with collectivism has been mandated, there remains sceptical tentative support and unabashed critics – encapsulating the tensions between liberty and equality. Our journey to this arrival has not been without our share of fledging growing-up pains – and there is merit to revisit the historical social and cultural contortions that have brought us to this day.

Growing-up Pains

Following Aotearoa/New Zealand's prehistory and Polynesian foundations, a period of British colonial settlement, land conflict and growth ensued, the outset of a hundred years plus of white hegemony and transit into a dual socio-economic polity – the precursor to unsettlement and a precarious adolescence. Our growing-up pains have yet to ease.

The impetus for British annexation arose out of a rapidly growing and uncontrolled flow of immigrants from its colony in New South

Wales. Guilt about 'fatal impact' on Māori motivated the Crown to accept responsibility and take an active role in the governance of New Zealand. The humanitarian rationale was to get lost when the busyness of colonisation overwhelmed events. Edward Gibbon Wakefield of the New Zealand Company had interest in fast-tracking settler immigration from Britain. February 1840, the first of the New Zealand Company ships laden with eager colonists were bearing down on Wellington. Company pressure forced the Crown's representative, Captain William Hobson, to act in haste, resulting in an inexpertly contrived, ambiguous and contradictory Treaty of Waitangi – incurring implications with which we continue to grapple today.

Largely unsuccessful, the Wakefield notion of smallholder, self-sustaining agricultural settlements gave way to pastoralism in the 1850s and 60s. An offshoot of the Australian industry, pastoralism established on the open plains and east coasts of both islands, to become the heartlands and drivers of the colony's economy, changing both the geography and economics of settlement. Regionalism and provincial parochialism prevailed and this was acknowledged with the establishment of, and governance by, six Provincial Councils. With wool and gold booms, the South Island was the economic and political powerhouse of the day.

Yet depression was to hit the colonial economy in 1870 – both wool and gold were in decline. Hardships brought by depression were no novelty to colonists, yet the 1870s depression was not a setback limited in time, scope and region but something more pervasive and deeply ingrained nationwide. The settlers for whom private endeavour was the natural order were forced to consider State agency to lift the economy out of depression. This was Colonial Secretary Julius Vogel's moment, facilitating increased immigration, the provision of large public infrastructure and communications (roads, railways, telegraph cables including inter-island and cross-Tasman), and establishment of the Government Life Insurance and Public Trust Offices. Venturing into spheres previously the province of private enterprise, Vogel set the precedent for New Zealand's penchant for State involvement in the economy.

The practical difficulties of pioneering had been a great social leveller. Yet come the 1880s it was increasingly difficult for working-class settlers to buy land and they witnessed a class of elite landed-gentry living wealthy lifestyles that reeked of social, economic and political privilege – political rule enabled by property holdings and plural voting. Eligibility to vote had been dependent on being a man owning property of given worth or paying rent of specified amounts for rural or urban residences. If he held properties or paid rent/lease in different electorates, he was eligible to vote in each of those electorates. Too, a country quota established in 1881, enabled rural electorates to be a third smaller than urban, making rural votes more powerful (the gerrymander stood for 64 years until the first Labour Government abolished it 1945). It was a three-decade period of time through to the late 1880s when Canterbury run-holders, a relatively small coterie of educated men who counted fewer than a thousand, enjoyed economic and political influence the likes of which no other group in the 19th century matched.

Adding to resentments were observations of industrial exploitation and the insidious practice of 'sweating'. Strikes and conflict had previously broken out in a number of towns, but attempts to introduce legislation to improve working conditions had been repeatedly thrown out of Parliament by the Crown-appointed Legislative Council. A Commission of Inquiry in 1890 revealed the use of this type of labour was, indeed, widespread.

Land aggregation and its social norms of landlordism and serfdom, and monopolistic industrialism, with its social norms of capitalist proprietors and sweat-labour, were exact examples of the excesses of capitalism and deprivation in the motherland from which most British New Zealand settlers were endeavouring to escape.

Privilege and poverty were showing themselves. The uncertainties of the depression turned to anger giving rise to a conscious reaction against these aspects of imported heritage. Desire to reform colonial society to one in which such privilege and abuse had no place, led to a groundswell of reaction against the landed gentry of the country and the capitalists of the town. A distinctive colonial society and identity began to assert itself. And, by and large, with exceptional hiccups, it would underpin New Zealand society for the next 100 years, until the advent of the Lange-Douglas Government in 1984.

As the railways expanded in the 1870s, the need for Provincial Councils waned and central government control increased. In 1876 the Councils were abolished. Associated with this period of transition to the 1920s came a shift of economic and political prowess from the south to the north – and the beginnings of a shift in the make-up of those with political influence.

Elections were on the horizon for 1891. In the towns the interests of both parliamentarians and voters shifted from local to national issues. A liberal grouping of candidates led by John Ballance, an Irish-born ironmonger who had lived in Birmingham, England, packaged a set of policy on labour and land reforms that won the overwhelming support of both urban working class and rural small farmers. The liberals won the day and so did recognisable political party factions begin to emerge in New Zealand politics.

Amendments to the criteria for suffrage contributed to the Liberal Party win 1891. In 1879 the property ownership requirement was removed and the franchise extended to all adult European men. And in 1889 the long-standing practice of plural voting was abolished.

With the franchise extended to *one-man-one-vote*, working men began to get elected. The Liberal Party drew much of its electoral support from the urban working class, as well as small farmers.

Prior to the Liberal Party win, New Zealand experienced its first major industrial confrontation in 1890 – a trans-Tasman, 8000-strong unionist action that tied up the ports for two months. Unlike the subsequent waterfront confrontations to arise 1913 and 1951, it was a bloodless affair. Union officials viewed their actions as defensive – a retaliation against the growth of monopoly capitalism. And they wanted employers to recognise that unions had a role to play in workplace negotiations. The unionists lost the day but it politicised labour interests – the precursor to the divergence of property and labour and their political representation.

Many major employers took advantage of the unionists' failure – they refused to recognise unions, blacklisted their members and slashed wages and conditions. In 1894 the Liberal Party, determined to foster the union movement yet find an alternative to industrial conflict, introduced the first-time world-leading 40-hour working week and compulsory arbitration law. The law legally recognised unions, forcing employer recognition of them, while it outlawed both strike action and lockouts by employers (it, too, legislated against the exploitation of child labour and established the Department of Labour to monitor labour conditions and compliance). With no significant stoppages for the twelve years to 1906, New Zealand became known as 'the country without strikes'. The arbitration system went on to remain a cornerstone of New Zealand industrial relations until 1973.

John Ballance and the incoming Liberal Party in 1891 marked the end to the elite landed-gentry rule of the pastoralists. They came into office with an avowed aim to encourage the subdivision of the large estates and counter absentee landlordism. Break-up of the large pastoral estates ensued, particularly in the North Island, carved up into small family-owned farm holdings. While the country's principal occupation had been small subsistence farming, its contribution to economic growth was minimal. This changed with the advent of refrigeration in the 1880s. Refrigeration complemented by expansion of the railway infrastructure, opened the way for export of meat, butter and cheese, and by 1891 the importance of frozen exports was second only to wool. In the North Island there was now a steady growth of dairying – and dairying was the first industry to benefit from government assistance and supervision.

Prime Minister John Ballance's term in office was a short-lived couple of years before his death in 1893 and replacement by Richard Seddon. Yet Ballance had founded a party that was to govern for 21 years, enacting a range of humane and innovative laws which were the precedents for New Zealand's social welfare politics. Seddon was Prime Minister for thirteen years, earning him the title of 'King Dick', winning five consecutive elections before his death in 1906.

The 1879 principle of *one-man one-vote* was followed by *one-person one-vote*, fourteen years later in 1893, when New Zealand became the first country in the world to enfranchise women. This was but one of a whole raft of law change implemented by the Liberal Party that was to earn the fledging New Zealand society its international reputation as an innovator of social change and admiration for its egalitarian prosperity. The *one-person one-vote* principle, encouragement of trade unions, and compulsory State arbitration between employers and employees, set the tone for other significant new laws including free secondary schooling, an old-age pension, enhancement of workplace conditions, and graduated taxes on land and income. Not shy of State intervention, the Government nationalised the BNZ when it faced failure in 1884. The State, possessing unchallenged primacy in public finance, introduced monetary policies with considered social benefit – increasing public works expenditure, absorbing unemployed into Seddon's cooperative labour scheme, and financial assistance to support closer settlement, encouraging families onto small farms.

Yet the turn of the century was to be the harbinger of deeply troubled times influenced by global mood swings – worldwide working-class interest in socialism and communism, two world wars and global depression. Political forces came into play that proved to be the origins of the political divide between town and country. The interests of property and labour diverged to the point where consensus disintegrated giving rise to sectional interests packaged and represented by two newly formed political parties – Reform and Labour.

The original 1840–1854 British Colonial Governorship was superseded by the establishment of Parliament in 1854. For near forty years subsequent, Parliament comprised simply of cohorts of those with similar provincial interest and/or personal opinion. Political parties did not form until the 1890s with the advent of the Liberal Party coming to office. This was the prompt for conservative opinion (landowners and the middle-class) to coalesce into the Reform Party in 1909, with a focus on protecting freehold ownership of land against a prevailing powerful movement favouring leasehold title. Trade union interests coalesced into the 'precursor' Labour Party in 1910. The Liberal Party now led by Joseph Ward began to splinter between those with empathies for the newly formed opposing Reform Party and the yet not fully formed Labour Party. The Liberals lost to Reform led by William Massey, 1911.

The Massey-led Government, representing rural and urban property, held little sympathy for city unionists. A clear working- and middle-class divide delineated battle lines for class warfare and the Great

Strike of 1913, the most shocking of New Zealand's labour history. New Zealanders shot at each other and beat each other up in a struggle that took place not just in the mines, ports and railway yards, but in city streets and parks.

While the Massey Reform Government prevailed and socialist militants were cowered, the trauma of the 1913 Great Strike had aroused class consciousness in the cities. In repeat of the 1880s, an awareness had grown that class distinction prevailed – privilege and poverty had again reared its head within a nation of people most of whom had aspired to leave it behind in their home countries. In its aftermath, moderate and militant unions alike coalesced to form an organisation to fully represent industrial and working-class interests under one banner – that of the New Zealand Labour Party, now the longest existing party in New Zealand politics.

The global economy, and New Zealand, slid into the Great Depression in the early 1930s, and Labour swept into power 1935. Putting the two non-Labour parties on the defensive, it prompted the Reform and Liberal parties to reconstitute as the National Party in 1936 – representing conservatism and pro-private enterprise. So were laid the foundations to our two main parties, Labour and National – a class-based, two-party political system, which dominated New Zealand politics until the introduction of MMP in 1996.

The woes of the Great Depression had prompted a change of mood in the working- and middle-class electorates. Unemployment was rife, people were hungry, and there were riots in Auckland. Desire for the country to review its social conscience, a mood for a new society and new political leaders were the impetus to the Michael Joseph Savage Labour Party coming to office 1935. In contrast to the trauma of the 1913 Great Strike, but in keeping with the peaceful political and social revolution of the 1890s, the rise of a fully-fledged welfare state was born in the late 1930s.

Savage died five years later in 1940, but his administration brought the country out of the Depression and, led by Peter Fraser, remained in office fourteen years until 1949. The patterns and institutions established by this first Labour Party long outlasted the party's period in power. Like the Liberals in 1890 and their twenty-one-year governance which set the precedents for our social welfare politics, the 1935 Labour Government set the terms of political debate and action for the next fifty years. The Labour Government was ousted by National in 1949 and National were to hold the middle ground for the better part of the subsequent three decades. But all governments successive to the Savage and Fraser administrations maintained and extended social welfare politics into the mid-1980s.

The Labour Party set about consolidating and expanding the social welfare politics initiated by the Liberal Party in the 1890s and at the turn of the century. Amongst other things, the Savage administration introduced the provision of: free health for doctor's visits, maternity services, hospital and mental health care; established the State Advances Corporation, providing cheap loans for farmers and home buyers; nationalised the Reserve Bank; and introduced compulsory paid annual holidays. Most notably, Savage is renowned for the massive State-housing programme he initiated.

Perhaps with the exception of Christchurch, the growth of colonial New Zealand cities was ad-hoc and haphazard with little regulation or planning and no over-arching responsible authority. In the 1800s multiple independent boroughs prevailed connected by roads built by multiple independent road boards. Land speculation ran rife, the housing market driving development faster than planning or regulatory measures could keep up. For those who could, homes in privately developed subdivisions were available. For those who couldn't, it was inner-city, high-density tenements which, by late century, were overcrowded and unhygienic. Again, the very conditions immigrants were endeavouring to leave behind.

It was these circumstances that sowed the seeds for future State housing in New Zealand. A blueprint for government intervention emerged out of the Liberal administration – low-density urban communities separated by greenbelts and connected by public transport. Yet inner-city, high density tenements, overcrowding and unhygienic circumstances prevailed into the late 1940s as the advent of two world wars and the Great Depression intervened and building of new homes slowed to a near standstill.

The building industry took off during the 1950s and 1960s, part of a post-war thirty-year economic boom extending into the late 1970s. The building gave rise to new worlds called suburbs, which in turn gave rise to supermarkets. Initially building went flat-out to make up on the backlog – then to cope with booming post-World War II immigration and the baby-boom. The majority of immigrants were from Britain. Hot on their heels came the rural-Māori migration into urban centres and the first great wave of Pacific Island migration. Requirement for more workers than could be found had us welcoming those from our neighbouring island colonies of Samoa, Niue and the Cook Islands. They arrived in their tens of thousands looking for high wages. Polynesian communities grew in the suburbs of most cities, particularly Auckland.

Post-World War II, New Zealand was one of the wealthiest of countries – 'the best little country in the world'. As quickly as new streets and new homes appeared, shiny new material products were filling their rooms. And it began to have spin-offs for Māori – their populace beginning a cycle of recovery.

Twenty years on from the signing of the Treaty, growth of the European population and its resources superseded that of Māori. Settler disgruntlement with limited access to land led to their calling for the 1860s land wars and land confiscations that followed. A century on from the wars, Māori sufferance had run unabated. It had taken its toll on a proud people – aggrieved by century-long, on-going loss of land, and endurance of economic deprivation. Māori had continued to live in villages on their own small pieces of land. Almost all were farmers or farm workers and were poor. In the 1930s and 40s most lived in substandard housing and overcrowded conditions detrimental to health and often lacking safe water. In the 1940s to 1960s they started to move into provincial centres then city suburbs. Young men and women left their villages to work for wages, to return home to share their incomes. Then began a more permanent transition. A demand for manpower in industries grew and the drift evolved into a migration as significant numbers of families uplifted themselves and relocated. Before the Second World War over 80 percent of Māori lived in rural areas. By 2013, 84 percent lived in urban areas, a quarter of them in the Auckland region.

Into the first decades of the 1900s isolation continued to reinforce local and tribal identity as per traditional hapū groupings. Tribe lived apart from tribe and apart from Pākehā. Come the 1960s, communities of Pākehā and Māori came into sustained close contact with each other, reducing the physical separation of the two races which had prevailed for 120 years. But, too, it reduced the physical separation between tribes and hapū. In colonial times, a Tūhoe Māori would have regarded him/herself as far removed from a Tainui Māori as from that of a European. Yet the process of urbanisation was to induce an awareness of 'Māori-ness' over tribal identity. People from differing tribal backgrounds learnt to cooperate to solve shared problems. New urban marae were set up. Māori discovered detribalisation could lead to a shared sense of identity. The term Māoritanga became popularised. By the 1960s and 1970s the race as a whole had acquired a view of itself as Māori – albeit a strong sense of tribal identity persisted.

After initial awkwardness between Pākehā and Māori, friendships developed through jobs and social contacts, leading inevitably to intermarriage. Yet of most importance was inter-tribal marriage amongst Māori. In their home communities, partnerships were based on kinship and locality. Mobility of tribal groups, and inter-mixing in a flux of work, money and the bright lights of towns and cities, provided young Māori with a gourmet selection of multi-tribal, good-looking, brown-eyed companions. The offspring from these partnerships in the 1960s were the first generation to grow up as urban Māori, claiming affiliations to more than one tribe. Yet many, in generations to follow, were to lose track of those affiliations, giving rise to John Tamihere, who was instrumental in establishing the Waipareira Trust, to support and represent the interests of urban Māori who could not whakapapa to a marae, and to a historic ruling by the Waitangi Tribunal in 1988 that the Treaty of Waitangi is aimed at protecting Māori interests in general, not just the property rights of tribal Māori.

The 1960s was the era of the Keith Holyoake National Party. My boyhood perceptions of the Prime Minister were that of a pompous, plummy-voiced man – apparently the outcome of elocution lessons imposed by his mother. Little did I realise how well respected he was nationally and internationally, nor his hard-working farming background, and reputation and relish for putting on his gumboots when needs required or when he found excuse to do so. 'Kiwi Keith' presided for nigh on twelve years. It was Holyoake who eased the wrench of our trade relationship dependence on Britain when it joined the European Economic Community. Since the advent of refrigeration in the 1880s, New Zealand had been Britain's farm and Britain New Zealand's factory. As Britain began to identify more closely with Europe, so did we begin to identify more closely with the Pacific.

Wealth and income continued to be shared between the middle- and working-classes more equally than any other country in the world. Mindful of the costs of maintaining our social welfare system in light of an enforced weaning from Mother England and unpredictable economic currents ahead, the Holyoake Government set up a royal commission which ran for three years 1969–1972 to determine its future viability. The Commission confirmed not only the worth of the welfare state but recommended the expansion of it – expansion from one that provided basic economic and social support, to one that would enable beneficiaries to take a full part in the mainstream life of community. It reported first to the Holyoake Government on the cusp of its ousting by the incoming 1972 Norman Kirk Labour Government. It was the Kirk administration that ran with its recommendations, doubled the family benefit, introduced the Domestic Purposes Benefit and established the Accident Compensation Commission in 1974. The ACC built on the Liberal Party Worker's Compensation Act 1900 – at that time a world first no-faults principle of worker's compensation for workplace accidents. World leading once again, the ACC introduced a comprehensive 24-hour no-fault insurance for all personal injury. As we embark into the 21st century we recognise the blurring and difficulty of distinguishing between workplace-induced chronic illness, and natural age-induced degradation of health. Bringing us to the proposed 2020 Green Party Poverty Action plan to extend the provision of ACC to an all-inclusive agency for comprehensive care, covering illness and injury – if we can get over our neoliberal sensitivities.

Changing Colours

September 2016, a young Frenchman frustrated by a four-day attempt to hitch a ride over the little-used road through Paparoa National Park in the middle of winter, lost the plot, and in a fit of rage, smashed the 'Welcome to Punakaiki' road sign. For which he was duly brought to account. Drawing on this incident, Anne Perkins made insightful comment on the wane of hitchhiking being symptomatic of breakdown of mutual trust and care – hitchhiking faded away overwhelmed by prosperity and self-interest[2]. After begging, hitching is an elementary point of contact between those who have and those who have-not. It is a basic exchange between need and ability to provide founded in a sense of solidarity – the same sentiments and ethos, at one time which, unquestioningly sustained hospitals, schools, universities and State housing. Nowadays, the notion we are there for one another seems a quaint old-fashioned nicety.

At one time the State was represented in the landscape of every New Zealand community, small or large, and played a leading role in the provision of infrastructure, investment in industries (including railways, energy and forestry), and community and social services (including post offices, banks, housing and hospitals). By the mid-1980s, governance and administration was entangled in a raft of historical legislation and a web of regulations, tariffs and subsidies with often contradictory purpose, leading to a general recognition and consensus that there was need for reform.

New Zealand's fourth Labour Government led by David Lange swept into power in 1984 with a landslide victory over the authoritarian Robert Muldoon. Lange's Government surfed a wave of new-found national sentiment to better manage environment. Indeed, the nuclear stand-off with the United States that immediately arose was essentially an environmental argument as opposed to that of pacifism.

But the clash of ideals with the USA galvanised a new sense of home-grown assertiveness. What followed was a wave of national euphoria as our 'David' took issue with the US goliath over the presence of nuclear-armed and -powered ships in New Zealand waters and then French arrogance over the bombing of the Greenpeace vessel *Rainbow Warrior* in Auckland docks. The Americans cranked down our status as allies, they and the Australians requiring us to remove ourselves from the ANZUS alliance, while the French blackmailed us to release, then gave medals to the State agents whom we caught and put on trial for an act of terrorism. Nevertheless, we waved our flags of conscience, swallowed our indignities and stood by our man.

After the adrenalin buzz came the hard graft. Lange's administration had urgent imperatives to reform administrative structure, and environmental and economic management of New Zealand. What followed was a whole re-evaluation of the purpose of the State itself. A maze of environmental legislation and multiple government agencies with different responsibilities for environmental management were dismantled. Specific environmental responsibilities were removed from those agencies and allocated to newly created ones: the Parliamentary Commission for the Environment, Department of Conservation, Ministry for the Environment and local government authorities. There is need to talk about the baby in the bath water before taking action on the current day consensus to trash the Resource Management Act. Most people's frustrations are not with the RMA per se, but with how local authorities deliver on its oversight. And those who complain about the machinations of local authorities need to be reminded that New Zealand is unique in that all such matters are handled by local *one-stop-shops*.

It was unfortunate that the sentiments for administrative restructuring, environment and economic management, coincided with strong currents of neoliberal thinking expressed in New Right politics in the Western world which saw the historical combination of commercial and public service objectives in the State sector to be root causes of inefficiency. Driven by the Minister for Finance Roger Douglas, what followed was that one of the most controlled capitalist economies in the world became one of the most open and deregulated. Perhaps with the exception of Chile, no other nation applied monetarist orthodoxy more literally and wholeheartedly than we.

Early 1981, in his inaugural address as 40th President of the United States, Ronald Reagan stated *government is not the solution to our problem, government is the problem*. And thus began the rolling back of the State in capitalist economies, the spearheading of neoliberalism and monetarist economics. Stark income disparities and social dysfunctions arose over the next three decades plus that just so happened to coincide with the rise of neoliberalism articulated by Reaganomics in the USA, aided and abetted by Thatcherism in the UK and then New Zealand's own packaging as Rogernomics in the mid-1980s. And if Roger wasn't enough, Ruth Richardson, Minister for Finance in the Jim Bolger-led National Government that followed Labour's two term office, hit us with Ruthanaisa. The 'Mother of all Budgets' conjointly drastically cut our top tax rate and cut welfare benefits. We bolstered the private sector while we massively reduced workers' rights to organise and represent themselves.

The reforms of environment and local government administration were dovetailed with New-Right economic policies. A cascading domino effect was set in motion leading to a decade of government department restructuring, decentralisation and commercialisation of State responsibilities, leading to the dismantling of the welfare state for which New Zealand was internationally regarded, and the destruction of social democracy as we knew it. After five decades of strongly centralised government, we, sitting with arms and legs crossed, went far beyond accepting the need to go into open-body position. In knee-jerk reaction, we suspended all judgement, disembowelled ourselves, and invited all and sundry to help themselves. Globalised capitalists hacked and hewed at our economy akin to Maui's brothers greedy and frenzied chopping up of the monstrous fish that Maui had landed. While other Western nation states made admiring and supporting *oohs* and *aahs*, not one followed suit.

There is no doubting that as a result of the reforms, the New Zealand economy today operates in a more business-friendly environment with better market-based discipline better attuned to meet the interests of the consumer, *no more need for 6 o'clock swills or Friday night shopping*. Yet, while New Zealand reinvented itself in ways that today benefit us, we lost a quintessential part of ourselves. There were great losses of employment and services from the closure and disestablishment of state agencies. Small town New Zealand suffered, and continues to suffer, prompting Michael King to lament that by the time it was realised that the costs of the policies in tearing the heart out of small communities were too high, it was too late[3].

Paparoa, a small rural community on the northern flanks of Kaipara Harbour, comprised a handful of homes, primary school, NZ Post Office, a branch of the Bank of New Zealand, a few retail outlets including a Four Square, chemist and fish 'n' chip shop. And a Dargaville District Council field office and mechanical workshop, the latter in which my younger brother worked and managed. While my brother's position was still available to him fifty kilometres away in Dargaville, the office and workshops closed their doors. So too did the Post Office and bank. Struggling with burdening mortgage interest rates, he uplifted himself and young family and joined the rural migration to Australia that had ensued. While Australia has always been a Kiwi OE travel destination and a workplace to save for a few years to set oneself up back home, the migration post mid-1980s set the precedent for significant numbers of Kiwis establishing themselves as permanent residents. Joined by another brother and his family, neither returned, with the result our immigrant family's tenuous roots were irrevocably severed.

In the late 19th century we had world-leading legislation that fostered the union movement yet kept industrial conflict to a minimum. In the 1980s unions were emasculated. No country in the OECD has experienced more dramatic de-unionisation, the result of which has been steady decline in workplace conditions, pay rates and workplace safety standards – compulsory paid annual holidays the only recognisable condition left untouched. Entrenched labour flexibility gave rise to a casualised workforce and precarious lifestyles entailing lack of security, leading to 21st century fixed-term contracts and short-term, on call, minimum waged employment. We were the first country in the world to introduce the principle of an eight-hour working day – eight hours work, eight hours leisure, eight hours sleep. In the 21st century we are amongst those who work the longest hours in the OECD, a long-hour working culture second only to Japan. All the while New Zealand workers receive one of the lowest proportions of a country's wealth in the OECD.

In the main, from the 1880s to the 1980s, most New Zealanders believed that a good goal for the country was equal opportunity and equal results. Notwithstanding the fact that within that equation for much of that time Māori were second-class citizens, and while racism remains a topical matter, we nurtured a predisposition for social democracy. At one time our welfare politics fully funded free education and free health for doctor's visits, maternity services, hospital and mental health care. The Government provided State housing and cheap loans for farmers and home buyers. When Britain joined the EEC and our social welfare system was threatened by the possibility of a funding crisis, the National Government of the day endorsed not just its continued worthiness, but recommended the expansion of its provisions.

Since the implementation of neoliberlism, State dependency has grown from the miniscule of the 1950s–80s to the insidious levels we have lived with since the 1990s. Home ownership is at its lowest since the 1950s and the number of people living in poverty in New Zealand has doubled over the past three decades. We are world leaders in developed country social and economic inequality with a growing underclass burdening health and social services, requiring a social welfare department the size of which New Zealand before has never known.

Our heart for investment in collective well-being, enabling personal independence, went awry in the mid-1980s – we lost the plot. The 1984 Lange-Douglas Labour Government led its demise. The political left went into shock after which a gleeful political right ousted Labour 1990 and ran full steam ahead with its sentiments. The thirty-five years subsequent have been an aberration in New Zealand social and economic history. The reforms have given rise to disparities of income, so much so, that New Zealand is ranked amongst the most unequal countries in the developed world. From a history of being one of the most equal, by 2010-11, on the Gini coefficient measure, we ranked a lowly 20-23 out of the thirty five OECD nations[4]. No matter the academic debates around Gini coefficients, differences between 'real' and 'relative' poverty, and growing GDP, stark inequalities prevail and the consequence of this indictment against our sense of Kiwi-fairness is the loss of egalitarian values – a tradition of which New Zealand at one time was proud.

Egalitarianism was a foundational value and component of Kiwi identity. Yet we now have a generation of people who know no other way of managing our affairs other than monetarist capitalism. It is a generation sceptical of regulating for civility or governing for social well-being. We are a neophyte nation struggling to realise what we have done to ourselves, let alone comprehend and learn from our experience.

CHAPTER 4

MAD HATTER'S CAPITALISM

Experience is a hard teacher because she gives the test first, the lesson afterwards.

— Vernon Law

Lewis Carroll's children's book *Alice's Adventures in Wonderland* is renowned for being one of the best examples of literary nonsense. It tells the story of Alice, who falls through a rabbit hole into a fantasy world of peculiar anthropomorphic creatures. It is a fantasy world where logic is extruded, shrunk, warped, turned inside-out and upside down. So, too, the fantasy land of unfettered neoliberal and monetarist capitalism – a land of peculiar anthropomorphic creatures trying to make sense of nonsense – deluded by the notion that any social ill or deficiency can be fixed by making it possible for someone to gain a profit out of it.

Most of us are not economists nor rocket scientists, but are, more often than not, blessed with common sense. And other than the disarmingly disingenuous or naïve, most can see the blatantly obvious; capitalist nations are haemorrhaging – neoliberal capitalism, akin to a pyramid selling scheme, does not work. If one thinks of money as energy, it is short circuiting. The trickle-down effect, by the letting loose of the private sector with the economy, is the figment of someone's fertile imagination equal to the fantastical surrealism of Lewis Carroll. As with Wonderland, unfettered neoliberalism and its contortions of narrative, structure, characters and imagery make for unaccountable mishaps and misadventures. Yet, like Alice, we have continued to flounder around and allow the Mad Hatter and his cohorts to play us for fools – while the smirk on the Cheshire cat grew wider, thinner and more cynical.

Dole Bludgers and Tax Havens

The neoliberal ethos packages itself as the way of enterprise, initiative and individual self-reliance with an open scepticism of the role of the State (hands-off governance). And there is much ado made of personal and collective need to break the 'dependency cycle'. Ironic it is that since the establishment of neoliberalism, State dependency has grown from the miniscule of the 1950s–80s to the insidious levels we have lived with since the 1990s. Neoliberalism created greater need to provide for increased numbers of dependent people.

This has been no crisis of welfare dependency. It has been a crisis of failed economic policies and a depressed economy. Yet, rather than take responsibility and view income insecurity as a socio-economic failing, governments have treated beneficiaries as scroungers, lazy, feckless and lacking ambition. Unemployment is viewed as a matter of personal responsibility and almost a voluntary state of affairs – the State provides benefits only if recipients behave in set ways. This often includes requirements to accept precarious employment or training, or otherwise lose entitlements. From this position it is easy to blame, demonise and manifest an image of the idle and irresponsible. Hence the justification for lowering benefits, making them harder to obtain, and harder to retain.

Based on the presumption that poverty is the product of personal moral failure, the beneficiary system became officious and punitive. It became depersonalised and institutionally desensitised to the extent that an entrenched culture of aloofness separated it from the realities of need. Interrogative procedures for eligibility became demeaning, and at worst incurred injustices. As opposed to welcoming those in need, the application process is designed to discourage the seeking of assistance. Current day practice is that prior to subjecting oneself to such scrutiny, one can only gain access via lengthy on-line questionnaires designed to deter applicants, before being able to gain an appointment to plead a case before a real person. Then one must negotiate a security barred door at the premises. It was the tragic shooting to death of WINZ officers in Ashburton, September 2014, that led to the tightening of security to gain entrance into WINZ premises. But surely the shooting begged the question as to what desperation would drive a person to commit such an atrocity. Treading one's way through WINZ procedures can be an undignified, humiliating and belittling process. I know – I have been there.

We live in a world where the philosophy of wealth redistribution has become that of an ambulance service giving hand-outs to broken people who make a nuisance of themselves, bruised and bleeding at the bottom of the cliff – in contrast to providing preventative medicine to healthy people and maintaining a productive economy on top of the hill. Treatment in the demoralised triage system barely provides sustenance enough to feed oneself, expecting a person on

2018 rates to make ends meet over prolonged periods of unemployment on a benefit of about $11,000 a year ($213.00 net per week). And for those who have argued it to be the lifestyle choice of freeloaders, I challenge them to walk in the shoes of a $213.00 a week leisurely lifestyle. Some were given the challenge early 2020. A significant number of a new cohort found themselves without income as a consequence of Covid-19. There were cries of indignation, *we can't live on that* – and that was at the newly increased 2020 rate of $250.00 a week – an Ardern-Robertson Government weekly increase of $30.00 equivalent to the total incremental increases of the previous decade. The new cohort was successful in their outrage and we now have a two-tiered system – one for those without income prior to Covid and one for those post-Covid – *yeah, right!* The positive outcome is a general consensus that unemployment payments are inadequate to meet the needs of those receiving them.

Idleness does not damage society. Really idle people may damage themselves if they dissipate their lives, but I would suggest it costs society much more to police and punish that tiny minority than is gained by forcing them to do low-productivity work. In keeping with this sentiment, the Christchurch Methodist Mission's critique of the 2011 Rebstock Welfare Work Group investigation, reported about 0.2 percent of those getting the unemployment benefit had received it continuously for ten years or more. And benefit fraud as a proportion of the total benefits paid was only 0.1 percent (in 2011). Yet it is such *dole bludgers* who are pursued with zealotry at the slightest whiff of scamming. There would seem to be societal consensus in support of this zealotry as the Green Party co-leader Metiria Turei discovered to her personal and political cost in her fumbled attempt to highlight the difficulties of trying to do something with one's life when 'choosing to live as a freeloader'. Just prior to the 2017 election, she was indecorously kicked-for-touch after her public disclosure that in her youth she falsely claimed Dependent Mothers Income when a solo mother and pursuing university education. Yet this is exactly for what the DPB and the ACC were set up to do in the 1970s in follow-up to recommendations made by the 1969–1972 Royal Commission – to expand the social welfare system to enable beneficiaries to more fully participate in mainstream life and community.

Research undertaken by Professor of Taxation, Lisa Marriott of Victoria University's School of Accounting and Commercial Law, shows we prosecute welfare fraudsters ten times more than tax evaders even though in most years there are many more cases of tax evasion. Potential gains from white-collar crime are high, yet when a serious financial criminal comes before the court, cases result with very little reparation and short prison sentences. High-profile examples include that in 1984 of MP John Kirk (son of PM Norman Kirk) absconding from New Zealand owing $280,000 ($945,000 equivalent 2020). He was extradited from Texas and sentenced to four months periodic detention. Former MP Roger McClay was sentenced to community service in 2010 for defrauding the Parliamentary Service, World Vision and Keep NZ Beautiful. Former MPs Sir Douglas Graham and Bill Jeffries were sentenced to community service in 2012 for making misleading statements in the Lombard Finance prospectus that resulted in the loss of millions of dollars of investors' personal savings. At stake, it is often argued, is the white-collar offender's good character, the damage to their reputation and their pending loss of position in society. In most white-collar fraud/crime cases, a mere 5 percent of the amount is repaid. In contrast, blue-collar financial offences are much more likely to be repaid in full.

While eligibility for and abuse of welfare benefits are policed with fervour, it is no secret that the bulk of the tax burden is borne by middle-class wage and salary earners. Discussing the Oxfam 2017 report on inequality, Catherine Hutton of Radio NZ noted the number of wealthy New Zealanders worth more than $50 million grew from 212 to 252 between 2015 and 2016. Yet Inland Revenue figures indicated more than a third of this group declared income less than $70,000. All the while tax havens for corporates and wealthy individuals have been enabled by governments worldwide. The international media began to release details in 2016 of corporations and individuals with large sums of monies stashed away in tax protected institutions about the globe. And a little self-analysis revealed that New Zealand was no exception. Finance institutions and governments, ours included, pleaded their legitimacy. Confirming the fact, neoliberal government administrations have aided and abetted tax avoidance for those wanting to avoid tax payments in their home-based economies.

The subtleties of difference between Mafiosi wanting to launder illegitimate profits, and international corporations, oligarchs, celebrities or other wealthy individuals wanting to avoid contributing their fair share of tax to society, is lost on me. Tax avoidance is a perversion and tax havens a cancerous blight on the functioning of civil administration. While we have tightened up our laws subsequent, let's forget the semantics – New Zealand has a history of enabling tax avoidance. All the while, our neoliberal administrations have constrained health, education and environmental protection budgets while continuing to moot further tax cuts in the misguided belief that the transfer of further monies to the better off will stimulate economic activity. This exact sentiment being National Party 2020 election campaign policy, to stimulate a post-Covid-19 economy.

Precariat

Newly graduated in resource management policy, 1986, my head was full of neoliberal thinking, commercial and public service objectives and root causes of inefficiency. And being an employee within the new Ministry for the Environment, the think-tank for the RMA law reform, I was party to the new infrastructural and environmental rationales that heralded New Zealand politics. Pursuing a career in resource management and environmental education I was ankle tapped late 1998. In a previous incarnation as a mechanical fitter tradesman in the 1970s my experience was one in which, in any English-speaking industrialised nation, I could leave a job on Friday and get another on Monday. Twenty years later, in the late 1990s, I was shocked to realise others viewed my practical skills, resource management policy and teaching experience, to be unmarketable packaged within a 50-year-old person.

Made redundant in a recessionary economy, what followed were fifteen years of under-employment and unemployment – the clichéd university-educated taxi-driver, wharfie, and helping hand and labourer for owner-operator businesses paid under the table. Middle-aged, and vulnerable to the whims of New Zealand's highly casualised labour force, I found myself amongst a new class of people identified and described by British research economist and author Guy Standing as the *precariat* – amongst people who live lives of insecurity, moving in and out of jobs that give little meaning to one's life. It was fifteen years lacking a work-based identity compounded by the frustration of status discord.

Neoliberlism is founded on the elements of globalisation, deregulation, unfettered movement of capital – and 'flexibility of labour' on which it is dependent. Labour flexibility comes packaged as job flexibility and wage flexibility. Job flexibility includes position status and skills-set. It enables employers to restructure and move employee positions within a company with minimal opposition or cost and requires employees to adjust skills readily. Such flexibility has enabled ease, speed and cost-efficient adjustment to employment levels in accordance with requirements for labour and expertise.

Reduction of employment security increased other forms of flexibility. It makes it easier to let go employees, reduce the costs of dismissal and facilitate the use of casual and temporary staff. The shift to temporary employees has been accompanied by the growth of modern-day employment agencies and labour brokers, which help companies source immediate expertise, shift faster to temporaries and provide contract-labour to meet workplace requirements.

Too, an often-overlooked aspect of globalisation is the way companies themselves have become commodities, to be bought and sold through mergers and acquisitions. Although long part of capitalism, what was at one time relatively uncommon, the trading, splitting-up and repackaging of companies, has become a distinctive feature of current day global capitalism. Commodification of companies means that any commitments made by an owner today may be of little credence with the owner of tomorrow.

A significant adverse consequence of wage flexibility, reduced employment security and protection has been the transference of risk and insecurity onto wage and salary earners. Not only has income insecurity gone up but the relative level of income received by most has gone down. And that income is more variable and more unpredictable. Those on precarious incomes, particularly if moving in and out of short-term low-paid jobs and dealing with the unfriendly complexities of the welfare system, can easily drift into chronic debt.

Precarious employment has become normal in nation state and global labour markets. Having temporary employment is not in itself problematic if a supportive social construct is built in accord to accommodate such a new normality. This has not occurred. On the contrary, the opposite has been pursued with a vengeance. Based on the assumption that there are jobs enough for everyone, the neoliberal ethos has been to demonise unemployment as the self-inflicted shortcomings of those choosing lifestyles as societal wastrels. Yet odorous hypocrisy wafts around – rather than viewing unemployment as a blight on society and a criminal waste of human potential it is cynically used as a policy tool for controlling wages.

With strong transferable skills, I applied literally for hundreds of positions up and down the country to no avail. The exercise – the constant despatch of CVs, most of which simply disappeared into cyber-space – was a process of despondency. Ageism was a contributing factor. On one occasion my WINZ case manager hung the phone up on a service station manager seeking a forecourt attendant who had turned away three others prior to me over the age of fifty (I was a sixty-year-old). I was a mature beneficiary for whom employment was second nature, and keeping with process to satisfy WINZ requirements was demeaning and belittling. It was an exercise in repetitive self-flagellation.

Within two years I lost my home and a subdivision project. A fixed-term contract in my profession proved to be tenuous. As time went by my professional skills lost their currency. I was over qualified and under experienced for positions for which I applied. Successful employment opportunities were low-paid and insecure – no regularity of work hours or security of income to plan and budget time and money. I sustained monetary losses from conservative, small-lump-sum investments (no Blue Chip for me) that under meticulous management foreclosed and paid out what they were able to salvage – albeit, over a 10-year period. Saving became an unaffordable luxury.

I am a classic case study proving that once a person has taken a temporary job after a spell of unemployment, the results are lower earnings for years ahead. When entering a lower rung job, the probability of upward social mobility or of gaining a decent income is permanently reduced. Short-termism took its deleterious effect on keeping skills current, let alone planning for, building and maintaining a career.

The New Zealand economy had decided to put me out to pasture, while it was sparing and begrudging in the grazing it offered to sustain me. I keenly anticipated my pay rise, and today greatly appreciate the regularity of income, when I came of age to receive the pension. I did find prior reprieve as an economic refugee – namely three years as an English language teacher in Thailand. My income tended to be flexible and unreliable, but I did establish myself in a nation that was prepared to let me have a life. Too, over the past ten years the nature of my contractual employment, voyaging on log-vessels bound for China and fumigating log cargo en route, required me to be out of the country to gain an income (until my company's insurance provider refused to cover over 70-year-olds). New Zealand wasted the skills I had to offer – fifteen years unable to fully participate in and contribute to community. A healthy economy cannot thrive when a significant proportion of their communities find themselves trapped in such prevailing circumstances.

My personal history gives evidence to the fact that discrepancies between *have-yachts* and *have-nots* grew as flexibility of labour became established. It begs the question what has become of our social-democratic egalitarian society when it valued one person's work effort at the 2018 minimum wage of about $34,000 – if lucky enough to have 40-hour a week employment – and another person's work effort in numerous million dollars a year (in small-time New Zealand no less!). When the Ardern-Robertson coalition increased the minimum wage to $18.90 April 2020 – an increase of about $2.00 per hour – there were exclamations of doomsday from the business fraternity. Yet there was a time in New Zealand when the difference between employee/employer incomes was about five- to tenfold. Today it can be 50- to 100-fold.

Home and Homeless

Our current day housing and accommodation crisis is a comic parody of our 1950s–60s self-anointed *nom de plume* as the land of the *quarter-acre paradise* – an example of marketplace failure unable to deliver on basic requirements.

The Key-English Government presided over the sale and running down of the government-owned housing estate and followed up by consistently denying there was a housing crisis – all the while continuing to pursue an agenda that matters, such as social housing, would be better entrusted in the likes of the Salvation Army. When belatedly and reluctantly forced to acknowledge a housing and homelessness problem did exist, they focussed on a blame game – bantering with the Auckland Regional Council about the supply-side of the housing affordability problem, as if it were only an Auckland problem. In the turn of events, 2016, the Reserve Bank acknowledged and informed Government, immigration flows were a primary cause of housing unaffordability. The Key-English Government pandered to a big voting bloc of Aucklanders who enjoyed spiralling capital gains, and it refused to address loose immigration. With the consequence that costs and availability of homes and accommodation became critical. Between 1979 and 2013, the average house price went from being twice the typical household's annual disposable income to five times as much, and in 2021, citizen homeownership is at its lowest since the 1950s.

Much of New Zealand's housing is not only expensive but substandard. We have families living in damp, mouldy flats for which they pay far too high a rent and who are paid too little in wages. In South Auckland, winter 2014, little Emma-Lita Bourne died, her short two years of life ending in a cold, leaking, mouldy substandard Housing NZ home. Maybe we have always had poor-quality housing in New Zealand. Yet, while the selfishness of penny-pinching private investors in rental provision is one thing, it goes without saying that slum tenancies enabled, provided and facilitated by government agency is an outrage.

While the tragedy of little Emma-Lita's death got public airing, it would seem she was one of but many. When acting as the Children's Commissioner 2011–2015, Russell Wills informed us that more than 40,000 children a year were admitted to hospital nationwide with poverty and housing-related illnesses, and that children died from them. Philippa Howden-Chapman, Chair of the WHO Housing and Health Guidelines Development Group, is Professor of Public Health at the University of Otago, Wellington. She is, too, Director of the Health and Housing Research Programme and the New Zealand Centre for Sustainable Cities. She has published prolifically on New Zealand housing and health issues. In 2011, prior to Emma-Lita's death, research undertaken by Howden-Chapman showed that poor housing was linked with an 18 percent increase in winter mortality in New Zealand – 1600 deaths a year from respiratory and circulation problems. Her work gave testimony to alarming rates of easily preventable infectious diseases, such as rheumatic fever, bronchitis, pneumonia and whooping cough. The report identified a grim reflection of lives lived without a regular supply of hot water, heating, a bed of one's own and easy access to a GP – pretty basic stuff one would say! I think more shocking was the insight that in well-off neighbourhoods, the infant mortality rate was the same as Norway and Japan, two of the best performing countries in child health in the OECD. But in our poorest communities, the infant mortality rate was at the bottom, ranked alongside Turkey and Mexico. Come 2020 UNICEF placed us 35th out of 41 countries for child well-being outcomes. Historian and author Stevan Eldred-Grigg noted people of rich suburbs lived to an average age of about 90 years, while those of the poorest suburbs died on average before 65 years. His damning conclusion – the end of the welfare state not only made the rich richer, but began killing the poor. Such facts starkly articulate the disparities of income and health in New Zealand between *have-yachts* and *have-nots*. I think it nothing but shameful.

Max Rashbrooke, author, journalist and a senior associate at the Institute for Governance and Policy Studies at Victoria University, has published prolifically over the last two decades on New Zealand economic inequality. His book *Inequality: A New Zealand Crisis* (updated 2018) was the first popular work to bring well-established facts to public prominence – and in so doing, trashed any residual pretence of an egalitarian society. The number of people living in poverty in New Zealand doubled over the three decades from the mid-1980s to 18 percent of the population by 2013. Family poverty housed 200,000 plus children. More than 30,000 people lacked a proper home, and lived instead in cars, caravan parks, night shelters, boarding houses or on the street. An exasperated Mike O'Brien of Child Poverty Action Group and Associate Professor, University of Auckland expressed frustration at the Key-English administration's neglect and denial of poverty and homelessness issues, stating that social scientists across a range of disciplines in both government and universities had for years identified causes and solutions[1].

These were matters government *chose* to ignore – chose not to address because of a misguided scepticism of the role of the state in macroeconomic management and the belief that left to its own devices, the marketplace would sort it – the neoliberal delusion that profiteering will amend social ills and deficiencies.

In the deeply entrenched entrepreneurial, capitalist economy of Singapore, housing costs are within everyone's reach. There, the State owns land. There, the State builds accommodation on a grand scale. Frustrating to contemplate we once did the same. The Ardern-Robertson coalition's attempt to address the housing problem has been lacking – KiwiBuild failed to deliver on ambitions. Yet, in contrast to the previous administration, it recognised and openly acknowledged a problem existed – and desired to do something about it. The post-2020 administration's credibility has been staked to those ambitions and has much catch-up to do.

Down Tools

Down tools, once the cue for a workforce walkout over some breach of a union agreement has become an anachronism. In this day we have fewer people picking up the tools and fewer places for them to work. Union membership has been in decline since the early 1990s – unions now but a shadow of their former selves, comprising an enfeebled 20 percent of the workforce in the 2010s. Industrial technology has reduced labour intensiveness. Too, workforce requirements have been reduced by the running down and moving offshore of our manufacturing and industrial base, facilitated by globalisation, freer trade and changes in finance laws. But the enfeebling of unions has in the main been a consequence of changes in employment law.

Helen Kelly, former Council of Trade Unions president, died of lung cancer late 2016, fifty-two years of age. She was praised for being the person who did more than any other in living memory, to restore the mana of the union movement. MPs paying tribute in Parliament broke out into waiata. She was the focus of a documentary feature by Tony Sutorius premiered in the 2019 NZ Film Festival.

For a hundred years, after the arrival to office of the Liberal Party in 1891, the union movement had been an integral component of New Zealand society. Its credibility was undermined by the Employment Contracts Bill and the divisive and ultimately acquiescent union response to its enactment in 1991. Helen Kelly was the daughter and protégé of her father, Pat Kelly, himself an ardent trade unionist and communist – he being an adversarial in class warfare and actively involved at a senior level in the Council of Trade Unions (CTU). If Pat Kelly had had his way the CTU would have rigorously fought against the enactment of the new law. But it was the more moderate and acquiescent CTU led by Ken Douglas that prevailed. To be fair, this response was in context of a general perception of union abuse of power, of which people had tired. There was public consensus in support of National Government intent to weaken and bring the union movement into line after a couple of decades of bloody-mindedness and dismissiveness of public interest which had prevailed in the 1970s and 80s. Of particularly public annoyance was the regularity of Cook Strait ferry-crossing strike actions at peak holiday travel times. Too, the construction histories of the BNZ building in Wellington and Mangere Bridge in Auckland were beset with long workplace stoppages.

The Employment Contract Act 1991 emasculated unions. It changed the default employment relationship between union and employer, to that of individual and employer. Compulsory union membership became voluntary membership and nationwide industry-based unions were deregistered, replaced by workplace unions. The near thirty years since has unfolded with a steady decline in workplace conditions, pay rates and workplace safety standards – the latter being a focus of Helen Kelly's efforts in an era of government complacency, particularly employee deaths in forestry and the Pike River disaster. Too, her endeavours taking the Government and the film industry (a la Peter Jackson) to task over the 2010 *Hobbit Law* – degraded terms of actors' employment contracts enabled by the Key-English administration to appease Warner Brothers' interests. To pour salt on the festering, the decline in employee incomes was the cue for Bill English when Minister of Finance 2011 to boast that New Zealand was at a competitive advantage over Australia to promote itself as a low-waged economy to attract foreign corporate investment.

We have witnessed a stealthy protracted repeat of the aftermath of the 1890 trans-Tasman waterfront unionist action when many employers took advantage of the strike's failure, refused to recognise unions, blacklisted their members and slashed wages and conditions. This instance was the precursor to our history of party politics – unionism politicised as the Labour Party. Following compulsory trade unionism in the 1930s, sixty years of growth into the 1990s empowered the union movement. The unions' ability to flex their muscles, and at times their exuberant willingness to do so, grew out of kilter in the absence of countervailing societal checks and balances. Today, we experience once again the flipside with corporate and financial interests having out-of-balance influence.

Perhaps there are examples to be found of workplace unions and their employer managements cooperating and enjoying productive businesses with happy workforces. But if that were the norm, the likes of Helen Kelly would have long faded into the woodwork – their contributions noted and shelved within historical almanacs. The fact Kelly earned her reputation and was honoured in the way she was, proves otherwise. Helen Kelly distinguished between 'high-road' and 'low-road' approaches to management. The high-road approach being where labour is in partnership with management, highly skilled, highly motivated and highly rewarded. Much like the prosperous industrial democracies of northern Europe – particularly Germany and Sweden, two of the few Western nations where manufacturing industries are the foundation of their robust economies. Workplace democracy is an essential part of Sweden's modern economy and is demonstrative of people being productive when they have a voice. For Sweden, trade unions are part of the solution, not the problem. In contrast, democracy in most Western countries ends at the office entrance or the factory gate. Workplace hierarchies can be damaging to business which gives rise to the low-road approach, prevalent in New Zealand, encouraging poor wages, poor investment and poor skills.

Current day business models and their profit margins are entrenched and premised on the availability of casual short-term or fixed-term, low-waged employment. By 2014 New Zealand workers were singled out by the OECD as receiving one of the lowest proportions of a country's wealth in the OECD – only Mexico, Turkey and Slovak Republic getting less. Too, we work longer hours for that proportion. Put aside any pride in the Liberal Government establishment of the first-time world-leading 40-hour working week in 1894. Reportage late 2016 indicated New Zealanders worked an average 43.3 hours per week – only one hour a week less than the Japanese. Our cousins over the way sat at 42.6 hours and our parents in the UK at 42.7. In contrast, Scandinavian nations (Sweden 39.7, Netherlands 39.1 and Denmark 38.3) keep within the ethos of a 40-hour week. Council of Trade Unions economist Bill Rosenberg observed Kiwi work hours rose steeply in the 1990s as the low-wage economy kicked in. They fell in the mid-2000s but have been rising again since 2010.

The fact remains the institutions of unions are necessary constructs to advocate for the well-being of employee livelihoods – to maintain and improve fairness and conditions in the context of ever-changing modern-day employment. Union disempowerment led to zero-hour contracts – an employee having to be on-call, and when, and if, paid minimal hourly rates. Zero-hour contracts are no longer legal and good riddance to them. Yet questionable practice remains, and so many New Zealanders find it very difficult to boast a fair day's pay for a fair day's work. To protect the more vulnerable the Ardern-Robertson administration has intent to re-establish nationwide award agreements for selected industries such as security workers.

The Ardern-Robertson administration's endeavours to improve employment conditions, increase the minimum-wage rates and work toward the longer term prospect of introducing a living-wage has been met by the business fraternity with anxiety. Opposition is premised on the very same logic used to argue support for the slave trade, *the plantation industry was economically unviable without slave labour*. The argument prevailing today is the business model on which contemporary New Zealand commerce is premised is unviable without minimum-waged precariat labour. Our cherished notion of a fair day's pay for a fair day's work seems to have got lost in the recesses and shadows of our collective memory. There is decency in decent wages. Poverty is nothing more than a lack of money.

Trade Training

And how is it that a nation of several million plus number-eight-wire-DIY-pragmatic adults is in deficit of skilled tradespeople? If our neoliberal governments genuinely support small business, why have sponsored apprenticeship schemes not been resurrected to provide trade-skilled people for them? Why do we continue to suffer trades skill shortages while we have lived with the levels of unemployment we have, and school leavers have difficulty finding employment? The devastation of Christchurch and its rebuild was an example of wasted opportunity for trade training. April 2014 the Wellington *Dominion* reported a shortfall of 5000 builders to meet demands in Christchurch and Auckland. Surely this is an indictment against single-minded focus on micro-operational profit and loss – entrepreneurs unable to provide for their wider marketplace needs.

Loose immigration has been justified to fill skills shortages. I have no issue with South Pacific nationalities arriving in organised workforce groups to meet seasonal horticultural need. Nor South American or European back-packers subsidising their New Zealand travel experience working the same, or as bar and wait staff in cafés and restaurants. The nature of the work – part-time, casual and minimal wages – meets their transitory needs, and fills a stopgap. Yet, Philippine nurses en masse is a different ball game. A large component of the nursing staff in hospitals and residential care for the elderly are today from the Philippines on three-year work visas – very thankful for the work, acquiescent about employment conditions, and able to meet our shortcomings. Yet, there was a time when our hospitals accommodated, trained and schooled nurses on the job, and I don't recall there ever being a shortage of staffing.

Similarly, the previous generation of government agencies such as NZ Rail, the Ministry of Works and Development, Electricity Department and the Forest Service were trade training agencies. They kept the New Zealand economy constantly supplied with a ready and trade-skilled workforce. Too, these agencies were overseen by those at the forefront of their professions, nationally and internationally. With the expertise and practical skills always immediately on hand, when a job needed to be done, it got done – none of this pussy-footing around with consultancies, and private providers, many examples of

which abound, delivering questionable value for money and result –
one of the more infamous debacles being the 2011–2015 Mount Eden
Prison Serco circus.

In more recent years, trade training has largely been delivered by
polytechnics, at cost to the trainee – you could get certificates in using
a screw driver and a hammer at one polytechnic, and a certificate to
use a hand drill at another. If a trainee had complementary
employment, they were allowed to use those tools on the job. I am
being facetious. But polytechnics and training institutions have
exemplified the failure of competition to deliver on community needs
– requiring bailouts despite on-going national skills shortages. At least
an acknowledgement of a problem with the newly created New
Zealand Institute of Skills Training – a single vocational education
provider responsible to administer and oversee trade-trading. The
Institute will free up resources, and programmes will be consolidated
improving consistency.

But what happened to apprenticeships whereby an apprentice is given
full employment under contract – supported by an employer, earning
and working alongside and being mentored by other tradesmen –
while attending a certain number of hours of academic learning at a
trade school (on the side) to complement one's on-the-job practical
traineeship. In contrast to executive salaries and expenses, current day
business models reckon staff wages, conditions and training as
negative costs. The model is not conducive to investment in skills
development as long-term benefit to a business, the wider industry
and national skills-base. Rather, ready-to-be-had skills are sort via
employment agencies, and when they fail to deliver, through
immigration. Our entrepreneurial marketplace singularly fails to
replenish and provide for its needs.

A Lot of Wind

Climate change is the mother-of-them-all 'tragedy of the commons' – a free-market externality, whereby the benefits of activities are privatised and the costs of externalities socialised. Sitting on our few rocks sticking out of the South Pacific Ocean, the Parliamentary Commissioner for the Environment's 2017 *Stepping Stones to Paris and Beyond* reported that our greenhouse emissions rose 64 percent in the 25-year period 1990–2015. The main contributors, dairy production and road transport. This is one of the worst records in the OECD. While our contributions are a mere 0.17 percent of the global total, we are the fifth highest contributors per individual in the OECD.

In 1972 the UN held the 'Conference on the Human Environment' in follow up to the Club of Rome launch of its analysis and publication of *Limits to Growth*. That conference gave birth to the UN Environment Programme, the global plan of action 'Agenda 21' and the Earth Summits convened every decade since[2]. The Earth Summit 1992 had a focus on climate change issues and how they could be tackled, and that summit launched the UN Framework Convention of Climate Change. Good intentions have failed to materialise. Forty years on practically nothing has been achieved. And if there is one single sentiment that teenage Swedish climate change activist Greta Thunberg has voiced, this can only be described as an inexcusable abuse of political responsibility. October 2018, the United Nation's Intergovernmental Panel on Climate Change noted we are currently on track for 3–5 degrees Celsius warming this century and clearly stated climate change is unquestioned. It is happening. The Panel sounded a clarion call warning we had twelve years to limit global warming to 1.5 degrees Celsius and stave off catastrophic environmental breakdown – *ten more to go*. A line has been drawn. I liked *NZ Listener* contributor Joanne Black's comment that an international recent year focus on single-use plastic bags and plastic straws, while commendable, is akin to tidying up the socks draw before an important exam[3]. It's called displacement activity – activity one engages in to defer doing hard stuff. In this instance, desperate search for technological fixes as opposed to addressing the root cause – our indulgent consumption.

American chemist Professor Will Steffen is on the Science Advisory Committee of the APEC Climate Centre in Korea. Alongside Dutch Nobel Prize-winning atmospheric chemist Paul Crutzen, Steffen specialises in the new era of the 'Anthropocene' and 'the great acceleration' beginning in the mid-20th century. Steffen argues climate change is a 'consumption' issue as opposed to that of a 'population' issue. Since the beginning of the 20th century poor nation populations have greatly increased, but their contributions to climate change gases have remained relatively unchanged. In contrast, OECD country populations have remained relatively unchanged but their contributions to climate change gases have hugely increased. And these are the nations responsible for 75 percent of global consumption. China and India are recent decade anomalies in this equation in that while high proportions of their populations remain living rudimentary lifestyles, their economies are home to ever-growing significant cohorts of peoples attaining first world standards, associated with increased rates of consumerism. Which challenges the specious credo that the way to address global inequality is to emulate the levels of consumption prevailing in the developed world.

First world nations live in an age of acquisitions – in a world where everything is available but nothing is valuable. There will be no change to the trend of climate change without some attempt to regulate and constrain our rapacious consumerism. There is no sign of that happening. And there never will be while unfettered neoliberal capitalism prevails. Prompting Green MP Golriz Ghahraman, in her introductory speech to Parliament, to stress our greatest danger is subjugation to corporate interests. Globally it will take many governments enacting laws and regulations in lockstep to block damaging behaviour before errant multinationals have no choice but to alter their business models. The climate change moment offers another opportunity for Kiwis to lead by example (as opposed to being *responsible followers*). In Ghahraman's words, it is time *to stand up and be that self-righteous little nation again.*

Have-Yachts and Have-Nots

The monetarist economy revolves around and is driven by debt. In little old New Zealand 2019, total debt stood at over NZ$462 billion[4] while the total money supply was about NZ$326 million[5]. Global debt sits at about US$253 trillion (322 percent of global GDP) while total monetary supply is estimated at about US$96 trillion[6]. China saved the day in the 2008 GFC by 'buying' America's debt. America owes China a heap of money (in the order of about US$1 trillion). Yet we now hear China is in debt to the tune of US$5.48 trillion[7]. How does this all add up? Who owes who what and where on this merry-go-round? There are Covid-19 pandemic distortions to these figures but the point remains. There is not enough money to pay the debts owed. And there never will be.

I think most scary is the size of the global derivatives market estimated between US$558 trillion and US$1.0 quadrillion. The nature of derivatives is such that no one can give an accurate account. A derivative is a contract between two or more parties that derives its value based on the performance of an underlying asset, index or entity. They are bets, *gambles*, made on future performance. Exactly the behaviour that led to the collapse of Fannie Mae and Freddie Mac mortgage-backed securities in the US and the 2008 global financial crisis that ensued. An out of control financial industry has been enabled to gamble with depositors' money, the root cause of the 2008 GFC. I think best described as 'phoney money'. The international financial system is nought but a house of cards precariously fearful of the next puff of wind *or virus pandemic* – a fairground scary ghost-train ride, funny were it not so outrageous.

To nurture and maintain trust in finance and economy, and play the game, the numbers are made to play musical chairs. This is what Auckland University Professor of Law, Jane Kelsey describes as the phoney economy and she succinctly sums up how it unfolded giving rise to our brave new world. Investments in FIRE (finance, insurance and real estate) are attractive, bringing in high, immediate and seemingly risk-free returns. People, companies and institutions with spare capital became increasingly reluctant to invest or reinvest in manufacturing, which can be prone to low profits, delay and risk. The simple and seductive logic is, if one borrows a lot of money, they could make even more from buying and selling financial commodities such as real estate, shares, currencies or derivatives. Hence, we see increasing prices for stocks, bonds and real estate – and climbing debt – as opposed to increasing consumer prices.

Too, restrictions on banks to lend for productive purposes alone were lifted. In the 21st century banks have been allowed to trade in financial products for their own profit-making. Competing with each other, the fastest way to maximise returns and earn bonuses is by speculative lending and arbitrage. Leading Gareth Morgan, pragmatic self-made-millionaire-entrepreneur and TOP Party founder, to express frustration there is a dearth of available funds for those wanting to invest in manufacturing.

Other than those of Gareth Morgan's ilk, fewer investors are interested in manufacturing or building a business to generate long-term financial returns. Managers of manufacturing focus on short-term outcomes and short-term activities. Companies restructure, sell assets, load balance sheets with debt. The easiest way to cut costs and increase dividend pay-outs is to reduce the workforce and real wages, defer investment, and outsource to other companies and countries.

Greater risk-taking is deemed necessary to achieve efficiencies. But the quest for profit comes at the expense of stable credit and quality jobs in the productive economy – with flow-on effects to the workforce. The share of added value, that at one time went to labour, has fallen. Gone are the days when wages would incrementally increase with increased productivity. While GDP has grown over the decades and finance posts record profits, employment conditions have declined, and wages and salaries have been squeezed. In this brave new world, the wider human costs are excused as collateral damage – excused by monetarists as *there is no alternative* (TINA).

Oxfam International's 2016 report into global inequality showed the FIRE economy to have nurtured sixty-two individuals, who at that time controlled more wealth than the bottom half of the world's population. Perhaps more shockingly the report indicated that in the six years prior, the wealth of the bottom half of the world decreased by 38 percent. While Oxfam reportage has its many critics, it is indicative of a massive increase in inequality that has occurred, all the while the post-2008-recession global economy has been growing.

In 2017, Oxfam figures showed 82 percent of the global wealth generated went to the most wealthy 1 percent. A handful of people were worth US$426 billion equivalent to the wealth of 3.6 billion people – the eight richest billionaires controlled the same wealth between them as the poorest half of the globe's population. One year later, January 2018, updated Oxfam data showed the world's billionaires increased their fortunes by US$762 billion, and the *Guardian* reported a record 357 newly minted billionaires as the wealthy saw their combined fortunes soar to an all-time high of US$9.2 trillion. Enough, stated Economist Branko Milanovic, City University of New York and author of *The Haves and the Have-Nots*, to end extreme poverty seven times over[8]. Then along came Covid-19, and mid-2020 the World Bank was forecasting 71–100 million people pushed into starvation level poverty hindering the Sustainable Development Goal to end extreme poverty by 2030[9].

The 'trickle-down' proposition espoused by monetarists is clearly witnessed as a blatant nonsense. Without social-democratic constraints, there is a natural tendency for capitalism to move wealth from the general populace to upper echelons. Bereft of ideas for finding productive things to do with excess funds gleaned via the globalised economy, cash accumulated by wealthy elite and corporations is used to bid up the prices of existing assets such as property, art works, shares, *even buying back their own shares to drive up their own share prices*, and build yet even bigger yachts. Self-serving behaviour. Author of *How Did We Get Into This Mess* and *Guardian* columnist, George Monbiot coined a word to describe this phenomenon *kleptoremuneration*. Adding there is no end to this theft except robust government intervention. With his trademark heartfelt yet cutting eloquence, he debunks justifications for stupendous inequality by way of meritocracy with 'if wealth was the inevitable result of hard work and enterprise, every woman in Africa would be a millionaire'.

Thus, global economic growth would seem, in the main, to be a good story happening for someone else. Same-same in our own micro *rock star economy*. Branko Milanovic noted the richest 1 percent of New Zealanders bagged 30 percent of all wealth created in 2017 while barely 1 percent of wealth went to 1.4 million others. This is not an issue of sour grapes for those who don't have yachts. It is a serious unproductive use of capital in which there are few new jobs created. Increased inequality is the result of money transferred into the piggy-banks of those who already have enough, while money is taken out of the pockets of lesser minions.

Contrary to the myth that neoliberal acolytes support small enterprise, they espouse the interests of corporate business as our salvation. They have unwavering faith in global corporations to create demand to keep local economies ticking over. Yet, if fewer and fewer people collect the proceeds of capital gain, and more and more people have weakened spending prowess, the slower money will circulate. Restricted spending power for daily needs weakens aggregate demand. The real productive economy is not driven by those at the top of our economic food chain. It is the collective of people with money in their pockets that drives capitalism and keeps it thriving and vibrant. Has this not been a prime learning of Covid-19 impact – small-business solvency threatened by lack of people walking the streets, spending money supporting local commerce?

The free competitive marketplace works effectively when demand exceeds supply. When supply exceeds demand the milk begins to curdle. Compounded by increased efficiencies to mass produce and distribute yet even more material goods, our economies are skewed toward excess supply. To counter the problem of oversupply, ever-demanding marketing ploys implore a cash-constrained populace to purchase, purchase again, then again – to keep with process and stimulate demand. Extrapolated to its logical conclusion, a continued trend toward more produce and less purchase cannot but lead ultimately to marketplace stagnation: akin to the last flames of a dying candle, the slow, self-destructive withering away of capitalism – the best wealth creating mechanism we have ever had.

There is a dearth of information supporting the notion that inequality stimulates economic growth. To the contrary there is a substantial body of evidence that high levels of inequality have hobbled economic growth. The OECD's December 2014 report played catch-up and supported a library of literature telling us capitalism was imperilled. The West's leading economic think-tank, long a flame bearer of neoliberal and monetarist orthodoxy applied in neoliberal capitalism, had a change of heart. Its 2014 report was an indictment of all it had long held as gospel. Not only did the OECD dismiss the notion of trickle-down economics but stated categorically it had *stunted* Western economies. The finger was pointed directly at the root cause – the increased gap between *have-yachts* and *have-nots*. They put figures to the stunting: the UK economy by 20 percent and New Zealand's by 15.5 percent – which the then Minister for Finance Bill English mocked.

Demise of Democracy

After thirty plus years of privatisation, deregulation, and cutting of public services there has been a shift in public attitude toward our *carte blanche* acceptance of neoliberal orthodoxy. Yet the fundamentals of neoliberalism prevail. *Right wing* politicians cannot see beyond privatisation and deregulation to solve problems. All the while, *left wing* politicians seem unable to implement change because neoliberalism and monetarist economics have changed the way we go about our politics. Growth in free-market public relations and business groups with financial clout have professionalised political lobbying. Conjointly public institutions and interest groups have declined in parallel with informative news media. These factors contribute to greater political influence by financial interests and decreased influence by social interest groups.

Long-form journalism about current affairs has largely disappeared and political coverage has been reduced to sound bites, buzzwords and preference for symbols over substance. Even our National Radio news programmes have morphed into *reality-radio*. At one time news media informed the public on Government thinking and activity, and provided discussion of politics and policy. With the advent of neoliberalism, government-funded news media waned and morphed into that provided by commercial operators. News gathering by commercial operators was funded by advertising and this coincided with the dawn of the internet and era of digital media. The provenance of the print media and their commercial viability suffered as their patronage and their revenues were eaten into by bloggers and other internet publishers. As competition between commercial providers increased, their focus turned to entertainment and celebrity news – their dependence on 'click' patronage grew while staffing and resources were cut back. As a result, information and accountability have been sacrificed. The profit-making mechanisms of digital capitalism have created a virtual reality whereby the truth is whatever produces most eyeballs. We have entered an era of 'news' packaged as 'click-bait' regurgitated so often that readers become believers.

Hand in hand with media focus on human interest, trivia entertainment and the loss of informed news, is the loss of a politically informed electorate and rigorous democracy. The 2017 international novelty of Jacinda Ardern and baby endangered her, too, to being treated and looked upon by media as celebrity gloss – as an attractive super-rock star for feminism – as opposed to a competent, articulate and heartfelt Prime Minister.

Our previous Prime Minister relished, thrived on and actively nurtured celebrity attention. John Key presented himself with boyish charm and the media packaged him as folksy, likeable and engaging. No one can doubt he was a man of his time – it was always the gloss of image he excelled at. Over his three terms we were witness to much theatrics, fraternising with the All Blacks, mincing on the catwalk – the personification of Wonderland's Cheshire Cat, head floating disembodied – there, then not there – then just as suddenly the entire cat sauntering close, seductive grin, casual sensuality to calmly state, *I never get involved in politics.* John Key resigned his Prime Ministership early December 2016. Accolades in the media abounded, he enjoying unprecedented popularity to the end. Seemingly one of a minority, I was confused, frustrated and confounded by his enduring popularity. On his resignation, the cynic in me immediately saw John Key – Merrill Lynch's former chief currency dealer – selling his shares when his popularity had crested and was about to trend downward.

The trend to an ill-informed populace has been complemented by the commodification of politics – both with corrosive effects on healthy democracy. When politicians are marketed and sold as brands, election and media expenses become enlarged and necessary. The costs of electioneering can cull worthy candidates who lack financial wherewithal, leaving the niche open for those who represent money, incurring repercussions for the breadth of political representation.

And candidates are endangered of being drawn to those who have the wherewithal to fund electioneering only to become beholden to them for political support. And, of course, monetary support from vested interests, whether from corporations, unions or other sector interests, comes with expectations of contractual and property-right arrangements that suit their agendas. The New Zealand First Party has good relations with the forestry, transport, fishing and racing sectors and a classic case is unfolding, that Party being embroiled in controversy around the handling of donations received from the fishing and horse racing fraternities. Leading to charges being made by the Serious Fraud Office against two non-party members late 2020. Concurrently, the National Party procedures, too, are being investigated. In both instances the underlying contention is the practice of splitting donations into smaller amounts to give the impression of different donations from different donors – and to avoid naming donors. The naming issue is sensitive in that it is not uncommon to accept donations from foreign interests. These matters highlight the need to review and clarify the whole party donation regime and the tightening up of disclosure law in New Zealand.

Canadian social critic, Naomi Klein, amongst others, has called this out as 'crony capitalism' – describing globalisation not as a huge free market but as a system in which politicians hand over public wealth to private players in exchange for political support. It is no secret that international corporations play one country off against another to avoid paying taxes, stymie trade unions and lobby against government regulation. International corporations have exploited countries with lower labour, environmental and human-rights standards to profit from them. Governments have obliged without addressing the distributional consequences of trade with welfare spending, worker engagement and educational support – resulting in chronic socio-economic insecurity and populaces that miss out on the benefits of globalisation.

While North American politics is the epitome of Klein's descriptor, New Zealand's democracy has not been exempt from its own trends of cronyism and plutocracy, and New Zealand democracy has been the poorer for it. It is a matter of record the Key-English Government had a penchant for facilitating favourable deals with public monies to oil the big wheels of big business. The eyebrow raising matter of the holiday to Hollywood set the context for the 2010 *Hobbit law* and tens of millions of dollars in subsidies to Warner Bros to buy Hollywood investment in New Zealand-based movie production. Other dubious politics included tens of millions of dollars in subsidies to Tiwai Point smelter owners Rio Tinto to maintain Mighty River stock values prior to its sell-off and creation as an SoE; overriding the sentiments of democratically elected regional councillors to enable the controversial Canterbury Water Management Strategy in support of big agri-business interests; millions of dollars to SkyCity casinos and a Saudi businessman to set up a sheep farm in the Saudi desert, *which remains just that – a desert.*

The controversy around the Trans-Pacific Partnership Agreement (TPPA) negotiations was not about a nation state which made stuff preparing to swap and trade with other nation states. It was about the secrecy surrounding negotiations. Negotiations were held behind closed doors, closed to most members of our Parliament. Why so? Because they were commercially sensitive, that's why. Leading to renowned economist Joseph Stiglitz's observation the TPPA was not about free trade but 'managed' trade between, by and for international corporations – and once again you and me missing out on the benefits of globalisation[10]. With the arrival of President Trump's Presidency and US withdrawal from the TPPA and the revised CPTPP facilitated by the Japanese, agreements were reached removing provisions that were contentious for New Zealanders with regard to Pharmac, foreign ownership of real estate, and the right of government to create law to protect national interests and limit corporate access (as opposed to proposed investor-state dispute settlement provisions enabling a secret panel of corporate lawyers to override the sovereignty of our Government and rulings of our Supreme Court).

Our supermarket duopoly and petrol supply companies are our most familiar domestic examples of managed trade between corporates. To address the matter on home turf, the Ardern-Robertson Coalition Government empowered the Commerce Commission to request supply of cost and revenue data compulsorily from companies. The market watchdog can now determine where profit margins are excessive. This enabled the September 2019 Commission's petrol-market study with follow-up implications for petrol supply reforms, and there is twitchiness for investors in the electricity, supermarket, building products and banking sectors.

From dubious politics to the dirty, it was author Nicky Hager who described in detail the jaded colour of our least-corrupt-nation-status. It takes the likes of Hager, one of a dying species of investigative writers, who is prepared to challenge the status quo and be vilified for doing so. Hager used the term *dirty politics* to describe political activity that was unethical – unprofessional endeavours to hijack and corrupt public debate. The mid-2020 imbroglio involving National Party President Michelle Boag and MP Hamish Walker was but one instance in a historical medley of National Party members dabbling in unethical practice.

Hager drew attention to highly opinionated commentators who engaged in the practice of deliberately targeting political opponents in underhand ways. Staff in the Prime Minister's Office, in cohorts with blogger Cameron Slater, used information provided by the SIS to undertake political 'hit jobs' against National Party opponents and covertly promote seat-selection for National Party favoured candidates. While John Key was personally not explicitly implicated, he was responsible for the offices of both the Prime Minister and the SIS and their clearly evident abuses of power.

Too, he was blasé about a series of emails detailed by Hager which former National MP Katherine Rich had sent to bloggers Slater and Carrick Graham. Rich was CEO of the Food and Grocery Council while sitting as a board member of the government Health Promotion Agency, 2012. The CEO of the Food and Grocery Council was in effect the paid lobbyist for Big Food (read sugar), Big Alcohol and Big Tobacco industries. The Health Promotion Agency promotes healthy living. Rich actively worked to undermine the board's agenda (of which she was a member) by ordering numerous attacks on public health scientists and professionals. Eminent public health scientists were incensed, thirty-three of whom wrote to John Key, the Minister of Health and the Auditor General to vent their anger. The Chair of the Health Promotion Agency and the Auditor General were satisfied that conflicts of interest had been managed and an inquiry was not warranted. Three health scientists and professionals took matters into their own hands and successfully sued for defamation; judgement delivered 2019.

A shift in our approach to regulating operators in industry and laissez-faire view of how investors and consumers should be protected led to situations whereby issues, for which in the past we have expected governments to take responsibility, were excluded in theory and practice – and with devastating consequences for people's lives and livelihoods. The leaky building syndrome, Pike River incident, Cave Creek, workplace deaths in the forestry and agricultural industries, and investment company mismanagement of funds (Bridgecorp, Blue Chip and Lombard Finance) incurring losses of millions of dollars of personal savings, were all consequences of hands-off governance – symptomatic of lapses in underfunded State agency and lack of oversight of industry standards, work safety and financial practice.

Too, there has been an abrogation of responsibilities for macroeconomic management. The Reserve Bank Act 1989 gave the bank independence, effectively decoupling the bank from government policy. The Act came into fruition allowing the Governor of the Reserve Bank only a single focus (the inflation rate) and a single instrument (interest rates) to achieve that goal – ostensibly a simple technical task that could be removed from the hands of politicians and safely entrusted in those of technicians with objective non-self-interest. The outcome was that macroeconomic issues were all but removed from democratic oversight and decisions about them left to unaccountable officials – bankers. In 2019 the Ardern-Robertson coalition amended the criteria to include unemployment levels. The difference this makes we have yet to witness[11].

All of the above matters and abrogation of responsibilities have contributed to an attrition of democracy. And the inequality gap has enabled economic power to concentrate into the hands of fewer people, contributing to trends of political cronyism. For over three decades we have collectively been hoodwinked by the monetarist agenda, to support a social consensus that has enabled elected governments to exclude themselves from, and leave, important decisions about the economy to the global corporate marketplace. When corporations grow in capacity, they, too, increase leverage prowess that can be applied against the State, making governments vulnerable. And, of concern, are often able to translate their disproportionate control of resources into disproportionate influence over political and economic decision-making: the rich being able to vey for, if not buy, patronage, corrupting political process – plutocratic capture leading to tax cuts for the rich, tax avoidance and evasion, financial deregulation, the prioritising of returns to shareholders and owners of large companies.

Globalisation as experienced by many is exploitation. When shrugs of indifference were response to cries of anger from people who felt abandoned, a sense of what's the point become entrenched. Internationally, the loss of faith in political leadership and rejection of globalisation has given rise to a new generation of opportunistic populist parties and leaders. We witness political crises confronting developed nations in the rise of xenophobic, neo-fascist parties and a fashion for governments with popular autocratic 'strongman' leaders in West and East Europe, the Americas, the Middle East and Asia. Such electoral choices are symptoms of deep deficiencies. In the shocks of the Brexit vote and the ascendency of Trump, the clear message is that the system is broke, let's smash it. I concur with the first – the second is Luddism.

I think there would be a small minority of New Zealanders who would not agree that Donald Trump has been manifestly unfit in terms of temperament, intellect and character for the office he has held. Yet there is a deeper matter of concern here. Donald Trump was democratically elected and did nought but what he campaigned to do. He presents not so much what is wrong with him as what is wrong with the health of American democracy. He has been consistent in that he continues to operate in the same manner in which he has pursued his life and which put him in office. He is reality-TV come real – the epitome manifest of the dumbing down of information and disregard for civil, social and democratic values. The corporate *coup d'état*.

No better detailed than by Brent Allpress[12] and his documentary *People You May Know*. Allpress exposed the activities of the Council for National Policy (CNP) – an umbrella organisation and networking group of conservative and extreme right-wing activists in the US. Comprising evangelical activists wanting to reverse the separation of church and State, white supremacists pushing for segregated schools, the interests of big agri-business and extractive industries such as oil, the CNP has been harvesting data to micro-target vulnerable individuals (the emotionally and mentally unstable) and attract them into right-wing politics. The churches target the un-churched, influencing them to vote for the people the churches want in power. With the long-term strategy to rewrite the constitution, twenty-five years of activity has successfully pushed the Republican Party further to the right. Allpress suggests the Trump administration's Covid-19 focus to keep the economy and schools open is driven by oil industry interest to keep people moving in their motor vehicles. Resistance to legalising marijuana and its use for medical purposes driven by those invested in and wanting to maintain the profitability of opiate therapies. There are large numbers of CNP members in the Trump administration. Giving truth to the refrain *capitalism killed communism, now it's coming for democracy.*

It is just too quaint a notion that the power of such wealth, as described in the Oxfam reports, can be constrained by you and me dropping a piece of paper into a ballot box. Economies and democracies cannot function with such debilitating distortions. International democracy is endangered leading to the 2016 *Der Spiegel* commentary on the identified need and urgency to tighten competition law and establish mechanisms, institutions and rules to constrain unregulated corporate interests operating within an unfettered marketplace which now threaten the viability of life itself. In other words, more globalisation in order to preserve the positive forces global capitalism represents and to eliminate the drawbacks. But there is a caveat – as with charity, this starts at home.

Surrealism Stuck in a Rabbit Hole

The dysfunctions above are not moot matters. They are cancerous symptoms of internationalised deep-rooted malaise including *super-rich* disparities, precariat employment lifestyles and democracy weakened by cronyism – within which many people flounder and tolerate smug smirks on fat cats.

As the decades ticked by with similar talking flowers with silly personalities espousing the same old same old, I got angrier and angrier. Anger arose when I heard people talk about the economy as if it is some wild and wilful beast beyond our ability to control – some natural phenomena such as a tsunami or earthquake that we have to stand helplessly by and watch wreak havoc. Let's get real – the 2008

GFC was a crisis of human folly. The economy, global or local, is a human-construct manipulated by people. If people break it, people can fix it. Enough is enough! It's not as if there aren't credible professionals out there seeing and saying it for what it is. At last a growing recognition of the fact and a change in the tone of politics in New Zealand – yet we await an outstanding promise for real transformative economic and social change.

Kick started by Ronald Reagan's inaugural speech 1981, the elements of neoliberalism – monetarist economics, globalisation, deregulation, unfettered movement of capital and 'flexibility of labour' – have enabled a minority of people to become super-rich. We have had thirty-five years of phoney economy whereby the production of goods and services (the real economy) have been subjugated by a financial fraternity that moves investments in and out of countries at whim, generating personal profits, siphoning off nations' wealth, all the while congratulating themselves as being wealth creators, when in reality are but cash accumulators.

With the release of the OECD report in 2014, I thought, at last, an analysis that can't be fobbed off as left-wing rhetoric or nostalgic hankering for a bygone era. The West's leading economic think-tank, a flame bearer of neoliberal and monetarist ideology, was dowsing its own rhetoric. No longer able to ignore the chest-deep evidence to the contrary, the IMF, too, had a change of heart. In follow up, the then head of the IMF, Christine Lagarde, gave clear warning the global economic recovery is fragile, weakening and highly vulnerable. I couldn't believe that the whiff of change in the air I sensed came to nothing. I waited with bated breath for the public discourse on how the *new* New Zealand economy could take shape – I was left wanting. The media let it drop and the murmurings were let to hush.

Then followed the 2016–2018 Oxfam data indicating significant distortions in global distribution of wealth continued unabated. And to emphasise again, these huge increases in inequality occurred all the while the post-2008-recession global economy was growing. And now post-Covid-19, up to 100 million people are at risk of starvation level poverty. How can we morally justify a distribution of resources that allocates on such a wide scale, so much to so few, while so little to so many? Surely we have constructed and operate a global economic order today that has become more unfair than any previous construct in human history. Yes, history is littered with aristocrats and financiers who lived privileged lifestyles in civilisations founded and supported on slavery and wretchedness. Yet those societies and economies were localised and even the privileged lived lives shortened and brutalised by warfare, disease and shortcomings of the technology of the day.

There are those who have long held the view growth in disparity of income is a non-issue; in fact a good thing, in that it serves as incentive to inspire minions to risk-take to better position themselves to climb the economic ladder of prosperity. This has long been the neoliberal rallying call sounded from the parapets for over thirty years. Early 2014, Thomas Piketty packaged 200 years of data in his book *Capital in the Twenty-First Century* and buried that notion for good. Once capital exceeds the real growth of wages and output, it rises disproportionately faster within the pattern of output, enabling exponential rises in inequality. In follow-up, the OECD clearly stated growth of income inequality *is* an issue which has significant negative impact on growth – and emphasised the redistribution of disposable income and reversing of inequality, not only has no adverse effect on economic growth, but in fact makes societies richer.

Those of us a little longer in the tooth than a mere thirties-something can reflect on New Zealand's most equal and egalitarian times and realise, they were, too, our most prosperous times. Epidemiologists Richard Wilkinson and Kate Pickett said as much in their 2009 book *The Spirit Level*, the subtitle saying it all: *why more equal societies almost always do better*. They argue a wide range of health and delinquency outcomes are worse in more unequal countries, regardless as to whether those countries are rich or poor. They ranked New Zealand sixth most unequal out of twenty-three rich countries. Five years later the 2014 OECD report showed New Zealand was the worst affected of all the OECD nations.

The *New Scientist* (13 July 2013) reported on research suggesting 1978 was the world's wonder year – as good as it ever was. And it has been downhill ever since. Ida Kubiszewski and Robert Costanza at the Australian National University, Canberra, devised the Genuine Progress Indicator (GPI) which adjusts GDP expenditure in twenty-six ways to account for social and environmental costs. They collected data from seventeen countries accounting for more than half the world's population to show that GPI peaked in 1978 and declined for the 35 years subsequent. Costanza is quoted, 'we are not making a social profit – growing inequality of incomes and environmental degradation are the biggest factors dragging GPI down'.

We have continually been beguiled by yet more tax cuts, while all important matters of social profit have gone underfunded: environmental issues side-lined (industrialised agriculture and water quality not to mention the ultimate failure of the marketplace – global warming); education becoming more expensive to deliver and receive (voluntary school donations and tertiary student loans and debilitating personal debt, and as has come to light post-Covid-19 – financial dependency on foreign students); our health system systemically underfunded (public appeals treating health issues as charitable causes and in run-up to 2020 elections National Party policy to establish profit-making privately-run Covid-19 quarantine facilities). Not everything can or should be run as a business enterprise. In an economy as small as ours and the geography of our islands, I never understood the making of strategic assets such as our ports, function in competition with each other. Even the concept of community is construed as a business construct. Schools are required to compete with each other, and I personally find it obscene profit be expected to be had from incarcerating people and providing care for the elderly.

Successive governments over the decades have chipped away at hands-on-government. Yet, law, regulations, standards and rules provide coherence to society. Regulation defends democracy – bureaucracy is a mark of civilisation without which the law of the jungle prevails. Hence, the law we witness and the previously noted toll borne by our citizenry as a result of laissez-faire governance.

Unemployment, low insecure wages, weak labour laws, slum housing are not the way to go. It adds up to a lot of people getting only the *gross* component of domestic product. I have grown tired of this never-ending tea party in a rabbit hole going nowhere. Stuck in a three-decade-long six o'clock time-warp going around in circles listening to unanswerable riddles and nonsensical verse, while continuing to switch places at the table at any given time to give impression of progressive change – all the while noting it was the Mad Hatter who contrived the switch rotation and only he to get the clean cup.

Ankle-tapped by the White Rabbit, Alice went into free-fall only to land in a circular room. There are multiple doors to gain exit from the room but they are all locked and there is only one key to a very small narrow door through which she is too large to fit. Peeping, she can see a beautiful garden with a sparkling fountain. Drinking a foul-tasting potion in a bottle labelled *drink me*, Alice gags and shrinks her body. Several mishaps follow but she gains access to the doorway to discover what she had perceived as a beautiful garden was instead brown and tangled – broken stone statues overgrown with dead vines. The fountain was empty and covered in a creeping greenish-brown moss. So, too, have we been seduced into gaining entry into the magic garden only to find the bountiful free-market *Shangri-la* continues to elude us. Yet we have been continually prevailed upon, *there is no alternative* – TINA, the resounding phrase of neoliberal acolytes.

Neoliberal and monetarist economics enabled finance to replace industry as the driver of wealth creation. As the old industrial economies were hollowed out, workers and their communities were told not to worry – the emerging services and knowledge economies would provide new sources of wealth. In the wake of the neoliberal revolution, New Zealand's Rogernomics, too, was full of the promise to transform our economy and bring increases in growth and prosperity across the board. Alas, the boost to innovation so confidently predicted by the authors of the reform has simply failed to materialise.

There is a simple equation in economics which says that without labour and capital, production doesn't happen. There was always plenty of noise when employees withdrew their labour – we never hear a squeak when capitalists withdraw their capital. Let us not be deceived. The global financial crisis of 2008 was not caused by outlandish public spending by social-democratic governments, nor by the conniving evil of powerful labour unions. The crisis was caused by the implosion of a house-price bubble in the US, fed by outlandish speculation, unsustainable and unregulated lending, deceptive and fraudulent accounting by financial institutions – footloose finance, greed and irresponsibility.

The GFC cost the world tens of trillions of dollars, rendered 30 million people unemployed and doubled the national debt of the USA.

Such are the consequences when governments wash their hands of the goings-on of unfettered markets and financial institutions. For political reasons, the US and European governments chose to assume the debts incurred by those institutions to prevent a catastrophic global collapse. And few were held to account. Corrupt and bankrupt banks and investment houses were given *get-out-of-jail-free cards*, asset values were maintained for the *haves*, fiscal austerity imposed on the *have-nots* (employed and unemployed), making poor poorer. The people who plunged the world into crisis walked away with their fortunes intact. To add salt to wounds, President Obama reinstated many of those architects and manipulators of the crisis into senior economic policy positions, ensuring that the American financial system remains largely unregulated to this day.

I have despaired. Time has ticked by and we have witnessed the same old collective, blinkered disregard. The marketplace can be truly free only when operating within well-defined rules – an ordered international framework of law, finance and trade. And because, left to its own devices its self-regulating properties are weak, there is need for embedded countervailing power. To save capitalism in the 21st century there is need for effective new forms of trade unionism, law and enabled public voice to keep it honest and sustain the demand off which it feeds. I vote we call it quits to this misadventure in this nonsensical, surrealistic Wonderland. In pursuit of a theory about the nature of the market, New Zealand society as we knew it has been destroyed. It wasn't that things didn't work in practice prior, it was just they didn't fit with new theory. Its exponents have espoused private profiteering as *the* only means to progress development – we have no other choice. This has never been the case. In hindsight the theory has been discredited and its continued pursuit is a travesty.

Alice discovered while running and panting alongside the Red Queen, that she wasn't getting anywhere. The Queen responded to Alice's query saying, 'in Wonderland it takes all the running you can do, to keep in the same place'. So too in neoliberal capitalism. The laissez-faire ethos is not only old hat and short-sighted, but the global financial crisis of 2008 and continued worldwide economic precariousness has proven it to be dangerous.

Neoliberalism globally and nationally is broken and going nowhere. Growing inequality is a malfunction which menaces vigorous capitalist societies, and needs fixing. As Alice in her land of make-believe would comment, it is *curiouser* and *curiouser* that we continue to tinker in this rabbit hole of fantasy-land-*con*jurery. Here, it was, we were introduced to the conductor of charades, the Mad Hatter. Beguiled we have been, for more than three decades underground – delusional in a twilight realm of confined space, little oxygen and time-warped surrealism. In order to free ourselves from the embedded systemic institutions of neoliberalism we need to arm ourselves with *Vorpal* swords, rein in the *bandersnatches* that run loose instilling some crash-courses in house-training. But the way out of the rabbit hole, to a world of fresh air, common sense and *Frabjous Day*, only comes with the killing of the *jabberwocky* of unfettered global capitalism.

Yet I remain unconvinced that we are any the wiser for our embrace of neoliberal capitalism. Hope beams with *Jacinderella* – someone with the political nous and desire to grab the rabbit by the balls and demand to be shown the way out to a world of fresh air and common sense. But we, and she, need more than fairy-dust – we need the mandate of a non-sceptical electorate to support impetus for truly transformative change. The 2020 electoral red-tsunami was enabled by a broadly disgruntled and fearful conservative electorate – disgruntlement with National Party disarray and fear of generational progressiveness being asserted in Green Party politics. In particular, endeavours to address climate change and concerns about impact on the economic viability of current day agricultural practice. Jacinda Ardern, aware of the trust that has been placed in her court, and being the strong consensus operator she is, will strategise to earn and keep that trust for the long-term. For better or for worse, there is propensity for conservatism to prolong the awakened and impatient generational shift desirous of urgent actions.

CHAPTER 5

YEAH, RIGHT!

Morning comes whether you set the alarm or not.

— Ursula Le Guin

The idiom *YEAH, right!* is formed of a double positive equalling a negative. Popularised by the long-run Tui Brewery advertising campaign, it has become a classic Kiwi phrase expressing doubt or disbelief – used to reject a statement outright or declare a heavy measure of scepticism. Whether or not the Tui advertising campaign of the early 2000s was taken from American slang, or vice versa, is of little consequence. New Zealanders have made it their own. The colloquialism is in keeping with a distinctive Kiwi humour, taking on a mythological status many identify with Kiwi-ness.

Kiwi humour is not the slap-stick put-downs of the American. Nor the farce, innuendo and double entendres of the British. Ours is more simplistic, openly honest and self-effacing. A sincere and humble humour in keeping with how we like to think of ourselves – yet cheeky: the cheek used as cover to an innate introverted nature.

While desirous to be included in the wider world there is need for the cheek to override our trepidation about standing out and being seen. There is no better example than the ethos behind the promotion of the fizzy-drink Lemon and Paeroa, originating from the small rural North Island township of Paeroa. A carbonated drink combining lemon juice, at one time, distinctively flavoured with mineral water from a local spring water-source. Its promotion, appealing to Kiwi humour, was advertised as 'world famous in New Zealand'. The phrase has since become popular, used to describe items well known within New Zealand but unbeknown to the rest of the world.

But, too, our humour can be cuttingly honest. I think no more so than the cynicism-laden idiom *yeah, right!* It is often applied in light-hearted banter but it has a sting in its tail reserved for matters of more serious import. When applied, the full-cutting cynicism latent within *yeah, right!* can leave a bitter taste. And the mother-of-all *yeah, rights!* has got to be reserved for the assertion that we have been participants in a *rock star economy*.

It has to be said the New Zealand economy was cushioned from the outfall of the 2008 global financial crisis by our Australian-owned banks – they, buoyed by China's insatiable desire for Australian raw minerals. Our tagging along on the shirt-tails of China's appetite for Australian ore was supplemented by China's newly acquired taste for milk powder. Nothing inherently wrong with satisfying China's taste for dairy, but it was the prompt back in 2008 for Winston Peters to name the spade: *we went wrong several years ago relying on one company, Fonterra; one product, milk powder; one market, China.* And we find ourselves today treated as economic vassals and patronised whenever we challenge China to conform to international law. The rollercoaster volatility of dairy prices over the last decade was eased by the significant uptake of tourism. While we sat back on our tourism laurels, we became reliant on overseas students to keep afloat the provision of our underfunded education institutions. Our complacency, dependence and vulnerability on both tourism and foreign students being acutely felt post Covid-19.

It drew my attention when pragmatic, self-made-millionaire-entrepreneur Gareth Morgan and social raconteur Gordon McLauchlan were singing from the same song book as Professor of Law and social commentator Jane Kelsey. The song sung being that we have had a shallow, vulnerable economy premised on a cocktail of spending cuts, periods of growth fuelled by financiers supplying cheap credit, immigration fuelled consumption, insane house prices generating never-before-seen huge increases in real-estate revenues, depressed wage growth and a persistently over-valued NZ dollar. We have arrived at the circumstance of a healthcare system and education provision at moments of reckoning, a housing crisis and infrastructure crisis, while living with chronic environmental degradation.

I do not understand why the 21st century global economy cannot deliver what nation states could half a century ago. In New Zealand, the information and digital communications technology industry has been a latter year emergent growth sector. Long may it grow. Yet we have hosted high rates of youth unemployment while bemoaning work-skills shortages used to justify on-going high rates of immigration. Productivity became reliant on immigration and the activity generated by Canterbury's rebuild. Fostered without forethought and planning, immigration exacerbated demand on under-funded infrastructure and social services. Today we are blighted by inadequate housing and a homelessness problem that didn't exist on this scale a decade ago. While we live with the lowest level of home ownership since the 1950s, those who can, use mortgages to realise property equity to fund consumptive spending. Property speculation is a key driver of income generation (the root cause of property bubbles) – and now a multi-decade over-investment in housing is distorting our investment patterns. All the while low productivity levels and low income growth have prevailed, New Zealanders have worked longer hours than any other Anglo-Saxon society, and received one of the lowest proportions of a country's wealth in the OECD.

A history of single-minded focus on ever increasing dairy production blindsided us to below-the-radar environmental problems – namely the parlous state of our waterways and quality of drinking water, and disregard for climate change. Chronic environmental degradation has been overwhelmed by startling socio-economic malfunctions. Infant mortality in our poorest communities had us ranked at the bottom of OECD countries in company with Turkey and Mexico. And after decades of neglect, UNICEF ranked New Zealand 35th out of 41 countries for child well-being outcomes. We are world leaders in developed country social and economic inequality with a growing underclass burdening health and social services, requiring a humungous social welfare department the size of which New Zealand before has never known. And making life difficult for beneficiaries does not reduce poverty. With the best budgeting skills there is often just not enough to pay the bills. Nor does getting a job necessarily solve the problem. The sum of which portrays a significant mismatch for a nation of people professing to the notions of fairness, intimacy and connectedness of an egalitarian community. These matters are malfunctions which invalidate any upbeat take on the state of the economy and the betterment of New Zealanders.

A rock-star economy? – yeah, right!

The spectacular increase in American income inequality was a major contributing factor to the global financial crisis. Yet the rich continue to ignore inequality, instead using their prowess to influence politically charged free-market and business lobbies. This has resulted in the switch of emphasis of State intervention in Western economies from that of making welfare capitalism fit for voters, to making voters fit for monetarist capitalism. Welfare reform has been used to get the unemployed to take low paid jobs. This was capitalised on by the deficit reduction and austerity policies of the post-GFC era, while the perpetrators in a very short period of time were back on-stream gifting themselves further bonuses.

While we and other governments act locally, Big Business operates globally. Everything is so networked that the debts of American homeowners led the entire world to the brink of economic collapse. And the upshot is that the world has become more vulnerable to crises. The monetary system has become decoupled from the real economy and money rockets around the world faster than ever. We have dug deep into a hole from which it will be very difficult to extricate ourselves. But we have to. There is need to civilise capitalism. The global economy can only recover if we succeed in pushing back against financial speculation and limiting the power of global corporations.

I take issue with twenty- to forty-year-olds begrudging the baby-boomer generation, how we creamed it while we could and now sit pretty, leaving younger ones holding the baby, to cope with a malfunctioning economy. Jane Kelsey introduces *The Fire Economy* with the note that the strong centre-right vote at the 2014 election indicated confidence in the Key-English economic status quo and a prevailing belief in TINA. TINA hangs around like a bad smell, I believe, because neoliberal, laissez-faire capitalism, is no longer *neo*. Men and women in their late-thirties and prime of life know no other way by which we can manage our affairs. And they have bought into the fearmongering and myth of a dark and evil past when labour unions ruled the world with iron-clenched fists.

I reiterate my long-time hankering for the day when the general consensus will again agree there are bigger equations involved in how we manage our economic affairs than our current day simple and single minded-focus on micro-operational profit and loss. Victoria University's Max Rashbrooke's 2018 book *Government for the Public Good* unequivocally confirms privatisation schemes and corporates in New Zealand have failed to deliver better public services at lower cost. I can think of no better classic case study than the debacle of the sale and repurchase history of New Zealand Rail. The establishment of our railways in the late 1870s significantly altered our political structures and what our farmers produced off the land. From those days on, New Zealand Rail was a major employer and skills-based industry which continued to move produce and people, lubricating our economy into the early 1990s. Sold to an American company in 1993, it was asset stripped and rundown to such an extent, in 2008 the government of the day decided to repurchase. Here was a strategically important infrastructure and service provider contributing to national wealth and social profit that has never fully recovered.

The time has come to tell the Mad Hatter and the March hare to take the dormouse's head out of the teapot – the dormouse can't breathe, for God's sake! There is something inherently wrong with an economic system that channels the spoils of economy only to the rich. There is something inherently wrong with governments that wash their hands of responsibility to manage wealth creation for the betterment of a nation.

Have-yachts and *have-nots*, the precariat, the hypocrisies delineating dole bludgers and tax havens have all been matters ignored. When Minister of Finance, there was occasion, 2012, when Bill English stated governments *don't have the levers* to combat inequality. Armed with the rationale of TINA, furtive glances gave way to a turn of the cheek. We have long argued at the margins ignoring underlying rationales – the classic behaviour of neoliberal governments washing their hands of macroeconomic issues while fiddling around on the edges with the micro to look as if they are doing something useful. Not unlike the situation when Alice's new-found companions convene on an embankment to escape her 'sea of tears'. To get dry a Dodo suggests a *Caucus-Race* in which everyone runs around in circles. Poverty and all the associated ills that arise within a low wage, 'flexible labour' economy, remain – nothing here that could not be fixed by a genuine liveable wage – simple as that – no further grand social policies required. That's how things used to be when we had a minuscule social welfare department. Yet, talking flowers with silly personalities have persisted.

We have had four transformative administrations in our political history: Vogel centralised governance; the Ballance and Seddon Liberal Governments shifted emphasis from private to public endeavour to address social and economic inequalities; the Savage and Fraser Labour Governments constructed a comprehensive welfare state; the Lange Labour Government re-forged economic freedoms, dramatically liberalising an open-market to rescue a stultified, command economy. The Vogel, Ballance and Seddon, Savage and Fraser administrations founded our attitudes towards the reach of the State in our lives and egalitarianism as a central tenet of our political culture. The ideology of the unfettered free market failed our predispositions, leaving in tatters our historical empathy for comprehensive, compassionate welfare.

The resounding mandate delivered to the 2020 cohort of Labour and Green parliamentarians is demonstrative that discomfort prevails with our normalising of social and economic dysfunctions and chronic damage to the natural environment. The change of tone to New Zealand politics that came with the preceding coalition rekindled a spark of optimism – that we had enabled another historically transformative administration. A refreshing shift it was, but the watershed reset of our political pathway for the 21st century has yet to show itself. To achieve the definitive break from the status quo and genuine reconfiguration of our economy and assertion of progressive transformative change, we must overcome the residual reticence and tentativeness in our collective heart.

A wake up call has been sounded – morning has come – time to start a new day – our *rock-star* economy has been a good story happening for someone else and it is time to realign with our better predispositions. Overtime to reassert our sovereignty, to realign our agenda and redesign a more secure and humanised form of capitalism. In her Looking Glass adventure, Alice is informed: *You're not the same as before . . . muchier . . . you've lost your muchness.* The Hatter poked her in the stomach with his finger. *In there – something missing.* Time to revitalise our *muchness*.

CHAPTER 6

REGAINING OUR MUCHNESS

The best way to make your dreams come true is to wake up.

— Paul Valéry – French poet

WE HAVE DRIFTED off the pathway of our nation's destiny and I have concern for the health of our economy, democracy and community – each in dire need of CPR. Yet, packaged and inextricably intertwined as they are in the real world, they comprise much bigger equations than our current day focus on micro-operational profit and loss. Cognisance of those equations is required if effective CPR is to be applied.

We live in a nation of very recent history, and as such, we are all immigrants or descendants of immigrants. Māori were not Māori when they came to Aotearoa – they were Polynesian. Pākehā were not Pākehā when they came to New Zealand – they were predominantly English, Scottish and Irish. Māori, as our first nation people, rightly claim the status of tangata whenua. It was to be a numbers game that greatly disadvantaged and overwhelmed them, as second nation peoples came for the very same reasons – to seek new lands to make new and better lives for themselves. It was for the same reasons South Pacific islanders established in the 1960s and 70s, and today, a fourth succession of immigrants from Asian and Middle Eastern countries adding to the flux – all with intent to improve on their lot. Whether your ancestry hails from the Tākitimu, the 'first four ships', or first generation World War II European heritage (as in my case), or a Cathay Pacific flight from Hong Kong, what we all have in common is the journey of generations over which the land has made us Aotearoa/New Zealanders.

In colonial times, every British immigrant's vision of the 'promised land' assumed everyone would have access to and ownership of land – the foundational root to our ethos for the 'quarter-acre home' with vegetable and flower garden and children's playground. Not forgetting free access to the natural environment and free flowing, uncontaminated water. Indeed, the Queen's Chain, unique to New Zealand, was designed to make explicit the notion that all New Zealanders regardless of class or money, had access to fish the rivers, lakes and coast and enjoy unrestricted access to the forests and mountains for recreation and hunting. Herein the roots of our traditional egalitarian ethos – opportunity and fair go for all and wariness of those who assume privilege. It is the same ethos in need of revitalisation to bind us together in a bicultural and multi-ethnic nation, actively involved in a community of Southern Cross South Pacific nations.

In their twenty-one-year governance (1891–1911) the Liberal Party set the precedents for our social welfare politics. Twenty-four years later the Labour Government took office (1935–1949) and like the Liberals before them, they used their fifteen years in power to set the terms of political debate and action for the next fifty years. The 1984 Labour Government, again the big reformer, shocked their left-wing support base with monetarist orthodoxy, yet set the agenda for the thirty-five years that have followed. Privilege and abuse have once again reared their head. The fault lines and chasms in our economic well-being giving rise once again to a conscious reaction against aspects of imported heritage *monetarist capitalism.*

The past three and a half decades have proven to be an aberration in our foundational heart and soul, values and politics. We forget, to our peril, that it is our interdependence which makes our independence possible and societies that invest in collective well-being give individuals the freedom and security to aspire, and inspire. Something has gone horribly wrong. We have accepted an account of our self-maximising nature and lost our common purpose. Our good nature has been thwarted by the most powerful political narrative of our times – an ideology of extreme competition and individualisation that pits us against each other, weakening the social bonds that make our lives worth living. It is time to tell a new story if we want to change the world.

Post-Covid-19 conversations have prevailed around our vulnerabilities in health, housing, education, infrastructure, environmental health, and the need to rebuild economic resilience. In New Zealand we teeter on the brink of indecisiveness, at a moment when we consider the pathway we wish to take. Teetering is a good sign because it means we are not quite sure we want to go where we have been going – we are unsure where we want to invest our thoughts and feelings to shape and structure the political landscape we want to live in. Because, let there be no doubting, the best wealth creating mechanism ever made is on track to destroy us.

Representatives of the UN Biodiversity Convention met late 2018. They spoke out about the crisis in biodiversity loss and drew attention to the fact that it is directly related to climate change. Just as critical as climate change, they lament the issue does not get the same media attention. Biological systems are Mother Earth's infrastructure – her nutrient, oxygen and water cycles, which support all her manifest microscopic and macroscopic forms of life. And on which we arrogantly forget human survival depends. Blinkered by egotistic, anthropocentric perceptions, our shortcomings make us very bad at scale – micro-biotic life too small to care about – climate change too big to get our heads around.

Extinction is simply the consequence of our uncontrolled consumerism. It is consumerism that drives 21st century climate change. Thus, there will be no change to the trend of biodiversity loss and climate change without some attempt to regulate and constrain our market economies and rapacious consumerism. There is no sign of that happening and there never will be while neoliberalism prevails. It behoves New Zealanders to acknowledge that unregulated corporate interests operating within an unfettered marketplace threaten the viability of life itself.

We live in a polarised world – poverty rising, populists responses, geopolitical tensions, hatred spreading. Climate change looms and biodiversity is collapsing. And neoliberalism offers no answers – rather, its continued pursuit is aggravating the problems. The Earth and its peoples are in dire need for revitalised nation country collectivism and global multilateralism.

International consensus is required to kill the *jabberwocky* of neoliberalism and the way out of the rabbit hole and *Frabjous Day* is nowhere yet to be seen. *Homo sapiens'* ability to collectively create myths, belief systems and behaviours have enabled us to dominate the globe. Humankind is now at a watershed moment whereby a new narrative for survival is required. Climate change requires international cooperation – the making of collective myths and belief systems to modify behaviours – and we need them urgently. No one nation, big or small, can go it alone. Responsible globalisation is required to tighten international competition law and establish new mechanisms, institutions and rules. New Zealand can contribute to that effort by calling on and making full use of our reputation as an honest broker. On home turf we need predator-proof fencing to keep the *jabberwocky* at bay (such as regulation on speculative monies). And we can wipe the smile off the Cheshire cat's face by house-training the *bandersnatches* that run loose (such as the recent year empowerment of the Commerce Commission to request supply of cost and revenue data compulsorily from corporations).

Max Harris is a Rhodes Scholar and researcher who worked as a clerk for Chief Justice Sian Elias at the Supreme Court and as a consultant in Helen Clark's Executive Office at the United Nations Development Programme. In his exposition *The New Zealand Project* he raised numerous proposals to revitalise our economy and politics, including to reassert independent foreign policy; forge our identity as a Pacific immigrant-rich nation; build capacity in peace and mediation; redress health and housing outcomes; renew our system of taxation and introduce a Universal Basic Income.

In her exposition *The FIRE Economy*, Jane Kelsey categorically states that to extricate ourselves from the entanglements of the monetarist spider web, progressive social and economic policies are not enough. She identifies the core pillars of the FIRE economy as the Fiscal Responsibility Act, the Reserve Bank Act and its narrowed *modus operandi*, and the Public Finance Act and its contractual mode of public finance enabling the privatisation of State power. These pieces of legislation have enabled what was once an integrated public service to diffuse into a web of public agencies constantly being reorganised and private actors performing public functions. She identifies a number of prerequisites for paradigm change. Namely: a new international economic model that replaces financialisation (killing the *jabberwocky*) with one that gives primacy to the social roles of economies; a platform of meta-values and ethics that infuses all areas of life especially business and government (which I liken to those espoused by Max Harris as the core values of Care, Community and Creativity); rethinking and liberating the role of the State with a socially embedded model of policy and regulation; restoring genuine democratic accountability; political leadership prepared to commit itself to this agenda; and an urgency in people's demands for change.

When the 1984 Labour Government restructured environmental administration, I found myself in the employ of the newly formed Ministry for the Environment, years 1986–89. I worked with a group of others in hazardous substances, and focussed on the development of policy for the management and use of pesticides. I left college at the age of sixteen and went through adult tertiary studies in my thirties, not going anywhere near a course in chemistry. And after School Certificate algebra in the mid-1960s, I followed up with university biometrics in the 1980s. Given generosity of heart on the part of my tutor, I gained a C– pass, meaning I could not pursue the subject further *thank God*. When in the Ministry for the Environment, I often contemplated my suitability for working in the subject area that I was. On reflection I was able to console myself I did have something to offer. Not being a chemist or scientist freed me from getting bogged in detail. I was able to stand back and overview the bigger picture and trends – about which, policy is the focus.

In the same vein, I now throw out a few 'one-liners' to address ailments more credible others have proffered before me, and about which I know little – other than, they resonate for me. And they boil down to the basics of a liveable income for every individual, and of need to actively love thy neighbour. All in keeping with Prime Minister Jacinda Ardern's address to the United Nations General Assembly October 2018, expressing New Zealand's commitment to collectivism internationally and domestically. She is desirous of the fundamental things – prosperity and fairness – to shift New Zealand into a place of kindness and well-being, the best place in the world to be a child.

I am of the view that the latter three prerequisites of Kelsey's – democratic accountability, political commitment, public demand for change – have shown themselves. But there is need for stronger popular assertion for genuine transformative change, to support the inclinations of the Ardern and Green Party cohort of ministers. I tentatively proffer my few 'one-liners' that could help toward Jane Kelsey and Max Harris's agendas – to extricate ourselves from the entanglements of the monetarist spider web. I have hope they resonate for you as they do me – founded on the basics of secure living and livelihoods for every individual within a safe, caring and sharing community of people.

Incoming Income

In the late 1970s, the early days of computerised mechanisation, there was growing interest in preparing people to manage greatly increased hours of leisure with which we were all about to be blessed. Futurologists were predicting reduced working hours for all sections of the community, menial to management, and consequential improved work–life balance – free time to dedicate to family and friends, personal interests, personal development.

The blessings never did arrive. In their stead, neoliberalism intervened with an ethos that held no countenance for such privilege being enjoyed by the plebeian. The outcomes of that intervention need no more but a summary reminder. Jobs were cut, the fewer full-time employees that did work held precarious positions under degraded work conditions. The increased profits accrued from computerised mechanisation were passed to executive management, investors and shareholders. Pay rates came under pressure and were reduced, regarded as a negative cost detrimental to the company and the economy. Whereas executive and senior management salaries saw huge increases and were seen as a positive investment in the company and economy. That is the process by which benefits and profits of technological progress have been captured by a relatively few people, and the process by which we have lost our expected era of leisure and our egalitarian society.

No better illustrated in its extreme than that by entrepreneur Jeff Bezos and his multi-national technology company Amazon. Employees work twelve hour shifts of monotonous physical hard work for minimum wages under constant pressure. With the exception of a 30 minute unpaid lunch break an employee allowance of 18 minutes off task is permitted for toileting, getting a drink of water or walking a little slower. Computer surveillance tracks employee movements and work activity – algorithms report on employees not supervisors or managers. The intensities of increased demand during the Covid pandemic, had employees protesting *we are human beings not robots*. Jeff Bezos accrues in excess of $13 million an hour.

We live in an economy with frayed social fabrics. The unravelled weaving and attempts at patchwork, now in danger of disintegrating further as we verge on another brave new world – that of artificial intelligence. The global economy is set to undergo a revolution spurred by machine learning that could be of far greater consequence than the agricultural, industrial or digital revolutions that preceded it. Our obsession with speed, convenience and efficiency may have become an unholy trinity. For what purpose are these brilliant inventions designed if not to serve us, support us, and improve our lives? Given the current management of our economies this will be a very unlikely outcome. What is likely is disparity will be exacerbated – that the super-rich will become super-richer. Fewer people in the workplace, earning even less, while the spoils of the technology accumulates to those with financial and asset capabilities.

The current day *have-yachts* are visually retarded by an overinflated sense of entitlement. They forget that every affluent person in every civil society owes their good fortune largely to the efforts of their forebears and the efforts of the forebears of less affluent people. Their health, education, positions, the infrastructure and technology that has nurtured them and continues to support their activities, has been enabled by societal effort, and cost to current day and previous generations. The *have-yachts* benefit from collective action, and therefore everyone has entitlement to the kick-back of the dividends of technological advancement.

We now witness the rise of xenophobic, neo-fascist parties and governments in Europe, the Middle East and America as a result of chronic socio-economic insecurity and deprivations their populaces suffer, missing out on the benefits of globalisation. With artificial intelligence we now have the portent for yet an ever-greater increased precariat exacerbating existing entrenched social and economic dysfunctions. An artificial-intelligence global economy burdened with a hugely increased cash constrained precariat will grind to a standstill. That is, if the guillotines haven't come out and there are lots of heads on pikes. The need to review how we distribute societal benefits more equitably has become critical.

In the mid- to late 1960s, I was in the employ of NZ Railways undertaking a mechanical fitter apprenticeship at the expansive Otahuhu workshops. It is true to say I was witness to much operational fiscal inefficiency. And there was, to say the least, much to be desired in employee work ethic. But with the insightfulness of hindsight, the workshops also served the role as a social welfare provider – this in the days when the Social Welfare Department was, for all intents and purposes, a non-entity to the humungous agency with its requisite budget of today. Yet, every inefficient worker in those workshops had reason to get out of bed every work day. They had constructive interaction with others in the course of their day's work and commuting. And they had money in their pockets, spent supporting local commerce. In other words, they had purpose and dignity to their lives, participated in and contributed to community and economy, and all the while, the railways delivered on creating nation wealth.

Compare that scenario with the lifestyle and contribution to community and economy made by those who struggle to survive on the current day unemployment benefit, who resort to scamming at best, and crime at worst. Let's not even mention social inefficiencies. Which system would be more fiscally efficient in terms of big-picture nation bookkeeping?

Gareth Morgan and Susan Guthrie did some number crunching on this very point[1]. They calculated it to be cheaper to do away with the Social Welfare Department as we know it today and pay every person over the age of eighteen an unconditional, tax-free, basic income – a living wage equivalent to the pension, as of right, regardless of whether a person is employed or otherwise. CHEAPER! – and that is not taking into account the resulting injection of cash circulating within the economy. Cheaper means it costs less to give this money away and reap the benefits of its circulation within the economy, than our current day arrangements policing a debased and demoralising social welfare administration.

Known as the Universal Basic Income, a standalone UBI aims to provide sufficient resources to enable a person to participate in community. Anyone who chooses to work over and above the UBI can do so without any added financial penalties. Interest in it is espoused by political factions and academics in Africa, the Americas, Asia, Europe and the Middle East. Modified diminished versions of it apply in Alaska, Brazil and Iran. Varied trials have been undertaken in Finland, the Netherlands and Namibia – two pilot projects in Indian villages are on-going. Other than in India, trials have remained just that and not been further progressed. Yet, positive trends were documented in both India and Namibia. The peoples of the villages spent more on food and healthcare. Children spent more time in school resulting in significantly improved school performance. It enabled citizens to partake in more productive activities – new business start-ups doubled, and personal savings tripled. It increased the community's income significantly beyond that of the grant amounts. The increase in productive activity in both case studies contradicts criticism that a UBI would lead to laziness and dependence.

In a New Zealand context, a standalone UBI could well achieve similar positive trends. And very importantly it would remove the stigma of unemployment. It is my belief that given the opportunity, every individual desires, and aspires, to be seen by others to be leading a productive life contributing, if not to the greater community, at least to their immediate community of family and friends. Our current day beneficiary system presumes that someone not in a job is not working. Yet a significant proportion of what needs to be done in society gets done by people who do not get paid to do it. The UBI neatly deals with debates around housekeeping, child-rearing, caring for disabled and elderly members of the family, and time devoted to volunteer and charitable work efforts. Too, in conjunction with reestablishment of universal free healthcare, it could possibly make our ACC system redundant.

Cash transfers lubricate an economy and liberate a person – enabling personal autonomy. They provide the social and economic security that enables an individual to have control over life's prospects. Because I had no family responsibilities, I pursued full-time tertiary study in my thirties and completed a Master's degree. I was enabled to do so, by weekly payments near equivalent to the unemployment benefit. In later life, the receipt of my unquestioned pension payments freed me from wasteful effort writing and despatching CVs that disappeared into cyberspace. Now I can use my time to apply myself to more constructive writing such as this book. While you may challenge the merits of my writing, I do find the outcome somewhat more satisfying and feel a more fulfilled human being for the result. Would you really deny me that?

A UBI-enabled, sustainable personal autonomy would be enhanced by other factors. Specifically, it would provide freedom to develop the talents one chooses including artistic endeavours and performing arts; enable people to move in and out of the employment market with ease (in keeping with the notion of flexible labour); enable freedom to choose employment that interests one; induce increase in pay rates in order to encourage people to enter the job market – all with the added benefit that when people feel secure they are more likely to be tolerant and altruistic *contrary to the international socio-political trend that prevails.*

Thus the logic and ethos is sound. It is clearly arguable that a UBI would be in keeping with the ethos of the Holyoake Government 1969–1972 commission of enquiry recommendations to expand social welfare agency to enable beneficiaries to take full part in mainstream community. An unconditional, tax-free basic income to every adult provides social and economic surety and enables choices about how to live and develop one's capacities. Re-establishing two key aspects of lifestyle lost over the past three decades – security and time. It is but a dividend to which all participants within our society are eligible. Local commerce enjoys a revitalised cash flow within the economy. And it's cheaper to deliver than that which is delivered by our current welfare provisions.

Should we run with its introduction, New Zealand would be the first integral economy to full-heartedly apply the theory and would be the focus of much international interest. TINA comes bearing and smelling of roses, here *there is no alternative.* But Morgan and Guthrie's support for a UBI comes with a caveat. An equitable redistribution of the benefits of a nation's economy and wealth generation must be part-and-parcel of revised tax policy.

Taxes and Death

If we are to have a coherent and fair system of redistributing income and wealth, it is necessary to conjointly redesign both welfare and tax policies. The rich are more adept and effective in protecting their wealth from taxation. Progressively, the burden of payment for public goods such as education, health and housing has increasingly been shouldered by middle-class taxpayers who don't have the wherewithal to sustain them.

Morgan and Guthrie's calculations for a UBI were based on the premise of a flat-tax. That is, no matter how much money a person earns, everybody pays the exact same amount of tax per dollar earned. Given current day dysfunctions with wealth distribution, I look askance at the idea of a flat-tax. Yet the notion to not discourage a person who gets out there and makes something happen for themself and the world resonates for me. I could be persuaded if there were checks and balances in place to counter our current day dysfunctions. The UBI is one of those checks, as would be a more rigorous system to counter tax evasion, which on the face of it, a flat-tax may enable.

The notion of a capital gains tax (CGT) seems to vex us. The introduction of one was on the Ardern-Robertson administration's agenda but it failed to make muster. Yet the arguments for seem obvious – to ensure that inheritance of wealth accumulated over generations does not accrue to a person simply because their parentage bore them into privilege. Amongst capitalist nations, we are one of the very few that does not have it. But perhaps it is telling, that even with CGTs, many of those same nations suffer similar disparities to that which we do.

Unlike most value added taxes throughout the world, our GST disadvantages those on lower incomes more than others due to the lack of exemption on basic foodstuffs. I have an intuitive preference for the scrapping of GST and the introduction of an 'automated payment transaction tax' (APTT) – a nominal tax on every cash transaction – the broadest possible tax base at the lowest possible tax rate. It is a 21st century technological application of the Tobin Tax. It would capture derivatives, eliminate substitution possibilities for evasion and avoidance, reduce to a minimum the costs of tax administration, and enhance stability of financial markets. Assume the tax was set at 2 percent. The tax on a $100 bag of groceries would be $2. The tax on the purchase of a $50,000 vehicle would be $1000. The tax on moving a million-dollar investment would be $20,000. It could reduce current day taxes on the less well-off and discourage the whimsical movement of speculative monies. However, there is debate as to whether one single nation could unilaterally implement such a tax given that foreign-exchange trading occurs globally.

An argument to extend our income tax regime beyond a single focus on financial capital is provided by comparing the tax liability of two owners of capital of equivalent value – one with a house, the other a bank deposit. Both receive a benefit. The homeowner deploys the house for own-use, while the deposit owner receives interest. Yet only the deposit owner is taxed on their benefit. It is the contention of economists Alex Staples and Geoff Simmons that a 'comprehensive capital income tax' (CCIC) could possibly address this matter. It could extend on our current tax regime to include 'effective income' received by owners of non-financial capital such as income from land, structures, plant and equipment, brands and intellectual property. All categories of taxpayer would be affected including homeowners, private owners of boats, aircraft and motor vehicles, and businesses owners. A version of it is applied in Germany, arguably the strongest economy in the world. Gareth Morgan has argued that as a result Germany has not had a housing bubble, but rather, relative housing costs have fallen over the past thirty years. Thus, Germans have benefitted from the strengthening of the economy by getting cheaper housing. We have continued to miss out on that benefit even while our economy *has been rocking*.

Whatever taxation regime we employ, the revenue gained needs to outweigh the costs of its administration within a New Zealand context: this being the argument in support of our comprehensive GST system – it is less costly to administer. Maybe you can tell I am no taxation expert. All I know is that it is a measure of how successful a society is, when you look at how people come into the world, how they live, how they die. There is need to devise a tax regime that improves on the distribution of our nation wealth, and on the delivery of health, education, housing, transport and care for the elderly – all those social public services that have been underfunded and let to slide for three decades.

Bank Rolling

In our world of monetarist economics, it is the banks which have the monopoly to generate money out of thin air and they who gain the profits. This is exactly what led to the GFC crisis and the need for state governments to bail them out.

Social credit has always been considered 'funny money', a little loopy and subject to mock – something the Social Credit Party has long borne the brunt of. And something leader of the Green Party in 2012, Russell Norman, endured when he suggested we print money to finance the rebuilding of post-earthquake Christchurch. He was mocked by John Key. Yet, printing money was exactly what the American and European reserve banks did four years earlier to save the day in the 2008 GFC – trillions of dollars of new money. It was, too, how the 1935 Labour Government financed its State housing programme. The State owned the Reserve Bank and used it to print money. Using the Bank's credit, the Government borrowed at minimal interest rates to build thousands of homes. In the years of a depressed economy, thousands of workers had jobs and cash in their pockets and the State found itself the owner of a very large income-generating asset. Too, the profit made by the bank was a return to its shareholders, New Zealand citizens.

I think the least we could do is resurrect David Parker's idea, when opposition spokesman for finance 2014, to introduce 'variable savings rates' for KiwiSaver contributions. The idea being to make KiwiSaver compulsory and enable the Reserve Bank to lift or cut the contribution rate to cool or warm consumer spending. This rather than raising the Official Cash Rate. It would mean the extra savings are kept by the income earner rather than being credited to the bank and term depositors.

And could not KiwiSaver savings be 'centralised' and serve as a slush fund for low interest Government borrowing, the repayments for which are profit to KiwiSavers? Could it not be used to finance a revitalised State housing programme? In direct contrast to the history of the Key-English administration's aversion to, and down-sizing of, our public housing stock, could we not emulate Singapore? Singapore has the highest rate of homeownership in the world – over 90 percent. There, State housing developments are publicly governed and developed, and purchases of homes are financially aided by a government fund. What is money for if not to serve our needs in such way?

The High Road

Joseph Stiglitz, amongst others, asserts that left to its own devices capitalism's self-regulating properties are weak and there is need for embedded countervailing power. To save capitalism in the 21st century there is need for effective new forms of law – amongst numerous other things, enabled public voice and trade unionism, to keep it honest.

To satisfy such an agenda and accept that unions have an important role in the conflicting rights of capital and labour, there is need to reframe employer–employee relationships – and this in a world where the distinctions between blue and white collar employment have blurred. Arguments to reframe are usually couched in the need for unions to modernise and adapt their *modus operandi* to fit with the times. But as the old saying goes, it takes two to tango – and at the dance halls Helen Kelly attended, there were very few people dancing.

To expand on those few numbers of workplace unions and executive managers enjoying constructive relationships and cooperative, productive and happy workforces, there is need for a determined managerial shift – to shift from the *low road* approach to management to that of the *high road*. To shift from prioritising shareholders short-term profits that encourage poor wages, poor investment and poor skills, to that where long-term business viability is favoured with the encouragement of labour in partnership with management – highly skilled, highly motivated and highly rewarded.

The Swedes have a unique system which the whole nation buys into – a centralised wage-setting process delivering both economic stability and international competitiveness championed by both centre-left and centre-right governments. It reinforces work ethic, entrepreneurial spirit and social cohesion.

The National Mediation Office, an institution unique to Sweden, sets wage benchmarks for 90 percent of all sectors of the employment market. The Office sets the benchmarks in negotiation with the country's main export industries and with unions. Wages are set to induce productivity that meets global manufacturing standards ensuring Swedish industry international competitiveness. And there is *Trygghetsfonden*, comprising ten job-security agencies which make up Sweden's 'job transition system'. These agencies provide expert support to workers who are made redundant to transit into other employment sectors. There is no legislation or public policy for *Trygghetsfonden* – it is entirely funded by private enterprise. The Mediation Office and *Trygghetsfonden* are constructs that depend on a tradition of high mutual trust and transparency in which unions agree not to contest wage-settings once negotiated, and to acquiesce to the loss of jobs when global market forces require companies to restructure.

The system is designed to shift employment from lower to higher productivity enterprises. Wage settings are set regardless of any one company's ability to pay them. Wages for the lowest paid are invariably higher than the market would pay, while settings for the highest-paid are lower than the market would pay which keeps the wage structure relatively flat and high. Those companies of low profitability are forced to raise their game to pay higher wages or they fall by the wayside. The result being the overall productivity of Swedish industry is boosted as non-productive business adapts or dies. Profitable companies for which the wages are affordable can invest their profits into further expansion instead of having to fight wage demands from workers wanting a bigger slice of the pie.

Trygghetsfonden is a private welfare system within the public welfare system. Companies typically pay 0.3 percent of their wage bill each year to fund it. It is the principal body that drives Sweden's employee 'transition system' coordinating counselling, coaching, providing and paying for certificated retraining programmes. A personal mentor is allocated to an individual for up to five years and there are no limits to the amount of money spent on that person to get them back into employment. It also tops up government unemployment benefits and trade union unemployment insurance schemes where necessary to keep a person financially viable. Eighty percent of workers are reemployed in other work sectors within one year.

If a company needs to restructure and let go jobs, helping the unemployed back into work, enabling them to improve their skills and making sure that they can meet financial commitments during the process has its economic rationale. Job security agencies are good for the employer because unions are willing to accede to layoffs. Too,

Sweden has a relatively small share of low-skilled adults and employers can draw on a pool of highly skilled people. And as education levels have risen and organisations make use of their employees' intellectual capital, steep workplace hierarchies have lost any residual usefulness – Sweden has the flattest organisational structures in the world. Another consequence of the system's focus on skills and competitiveness is that unions are up with the play, pro-market and pro-globalisation. The traditional trade union demand for job security has been replaced by demand for transition security – demand for investment in education and training and 'security of employability' rather than protection of existing jobs.

These factors are complemented by State-funded family policies that enable women to combine work with having a family, and enable men to share childcare responsibilities. Founded on the notion that gender discrimination is economically inefficient, accessible and heavily subsidised childcare facilities are complemented by generous allocations of parental leave up to eight years of age, and child sick leave up to twelve years of age. These provisions are seen as essential to achieving equality, as well as making economic sense by allowing women to maintain the currency of their professional skills and pursue coherent careers.

Herein proof the State can play a useful if not an essential role in economic affairs, in collaboration with unions and private enterprise. While Swedes adhere to the principles of the marketplace, including competition and free trade, they do not suffer the Alice in Wonderland belief that markets are self-regulatory and politics should be all about deregulation, tax cuts and paring back the State. They recognise need for regulated capitalism focussed on generating social benefit and nation economic wealth. They deal with job loss in a highly creative, humane and far-sighted way through the transition system.

Can we not be inspired by Sweden? Cannot motivated government agency, in cohorts with re-enabled democratic unionism and an enlightened private sector, devise institutions and process to centralise wage-setting and invest in a supportive social construct to ensure security of employability? Can we reimagine setting standardised pay rates for particular genres of employment and industry that similarly apply in a high-country South Island sheep station as they do in Auckland? As opposed to demonising unemployment, can we imagine an employer-funded *Trygghetsfonden* that invests in employee re-education and retraining to up-skill individuals, raise the calibre of the workforce skills-base, and build a pool of up-to-the-play highly skilled people on which employers can draw? Our entrepreneurs taking responsibility to provide for their own marketplace needs, eliminating their perennial shortfalls and calls for ready-to-be-had skills via immigration to maintain our economy or begin new enterprise.

A Third Place

My experience of childhood was growing up in villages, some smaller some larger than others. It goes without saying village life lived in 1950–60s rural New Zealand was a little bland. It was, as I came of teen age, the stable, secure, quiet and comfortable life I was desperate to escape. Yet while conservative outlooks and mores reigned, it was, too, the epitome of a simpler, happier, less conflict-ridden place and time – a friendly cohesive society. The door of every house was open to every child. My villages are places and circumstances that physically no longer exist. Ohura and Kaingaroa are emaciated economic remnants of their past selves. Riverhead and Woodhill Forest Headquarter villages, phantom landscapes. Yet they were where I experienced community and some sense of tūrangawaewae – an intrinsic part of me, yet forever ephemeral. And to this day I have never replaced the sense of security and belonging bestowed on me when a part of those communities, perhaps lending toward the adult Bohemian lifestyle I have led.

My personal story is of one who identifies very strongly with New Zealand landscape and with being Pākehā and cannot imagine living for an indefinite period of time in another country without refreshing my New Zealand identity. Yet, I have never quite fitted within Kiwi social culture. My fate has been to constantly yearn for more in life than what has been on offer at home. The days of buckets of tasteless beer washed down with Gregg's instant coffee have thankfully morphed into a café culture and selections of boutique beer and pinot gris as tasteful alternatives. The era of rugby, racing and beer has been diluted with a little wine, women and song. I have come to realise that this is always what I have sought and what New Zealand lacked – sensual street life, the likes to be found in Mediterranean, Central and South American and Asian cultures. Latin Americans and Asians are always a little perplexed when first arriving and venturing out into the streets – *why do things start closing at 5pm?* – until they have established a home-base network and discover that a little of what they seek can be found in the backyard of people's homes around the barbecue.

Bangkok is a sprawling, chaotic 21st-century South-East Asian city of 10 million people. It is exasperatingly overwhelming and disorientating but there is magic to be found in the living of it. No part of the city is purely commercial or residential. Tenement buildings line the *soi*, housing people and their commerce: engineering workshops, hair salons, convenience stores, internet cafes, many of them reinforced by the extension of private roof canopies over public thoroughfares – their interiors opening directly onto the pavements which are appropriated for commerce and as extended living rooms. During the course of a day, the walk of a *soi* is to experience a cauldron of food-stalls and hawkers with mobile carts flogging all manner of goods. And, of course, the ubiquitous noodle stand is on the curb nearby. Mobile portable kitchens set up with a few tables and stools wherever a likely group of customers can be found.

Of an evening, children frolic. *Motosai* fly by. Young men play soccer and *tdu glur* in vacant lots. People socialise sharing food and drink. There, an open-air restaurant, beer or karaoke bar, splendorous with fairy lights, blaring Isaan folk music – friendly venues where neighbours sing, drink and hang out with the staff. The street markets, mobile vendors and makeshift bars enliven busy thoroughfares – they provide texture, sound, colour, aromas and vibrancy to the chaotic daily drama of life that is Bangkok, without which a neighbourhood would be soulless and drab. Clean up a *soi* and it dies.

Bangkok requires time to discover her essence. Perhaps Barcelona and its Mediterranean culture would be preferred, comprising five and a half million people enriched by Gaudi architecture. Its residential and city areas packed with squares, plazas, cafés, restaurants, corner stores, small parks and street-side seating – spaces to meet, gather and linger and venues for impromptu street and performing arts. All within walking distance where people are to be found all hours of the day and night – youth, elderly, family groups – socialising or just hanging-out to see and be seen.

While contrastingly different, what both cities offer is the *third place* evident in many of the unplanned, ad-hoc cities of Europe and Asia, and what makes them so enchanting and enjoyable to experience – where it is evident that people come alive and enjoy living in them. They are places accessible, free or cheap for all-and-sundry *perhaps a little too scary for those who enjoy their gated enclaves.* Yet New

Zealanders fear the urban intensification that would enable *third places* in the design of our residential and urban environments. Instead, we have our *first place* (our homes) and we have our *second place* (our work) and highly efficient road networks between, consuming huge amounts of space, to move us as quickly as possible, with neither a tarry on the way, returning us to the inbuilt garage with access to the carpeted living room *lest we be affected by the elements that run riot in nature outside.* The lacking substantial *third place* is where community life is vibrant and active – that where we relax in public, encounter the familiar faces of people we know, friendly faces of new acquaintances and where everyone is up for a yarn.

New Zealand cities and townships are largely bereft of any sense of interactive community – there are examples of localised pockets, such as Aro and Cuba Streets in central Wellington and Devonport on the North Shore of Auckland. But in the main, they are mundane suburbs located around central commercial hubs, in many cases drab and dying. Ribbon development and urban sprawl carved-up by road networks are antithesis to vibrant communities.

And to boot, we are losing our most productive lands to continued urban spread and lifestyle-block fragmentation. Versatile lands of high-class food producing soils comprise just over 5 percent of the total New Zealand landscape. The number of lifestyle blocks increased sharply in the last two decades averaging 5800 new blocks a year since 1998, today having consumed 35 percent of Auckland's versatile lands. It is time this issue came out of the 'too hard box'. We can't just keep burying prime agricultural and horticultural land under concrete and tarmac to satisfy speculator and property developers demand to grow evermore *McMansions*. I don't believe it to be 'market' driven. There is a bigger market, a larger proportion of the populace who are want-to-be homeowners yet unable to even secure safe, basic accommodation.

Too, our revered free market fails to provide communities to live and socialise within. Other than sterile air-conditioned chrome and glass shopping malls, the best it can do are insulated, gated enclaves that exclude and segregate. And the elderly are conveniently tided-up in safe, self-contained enclosures, out of sight and mind so not to perturb our daily busy-ness. Yet there are notions inherent within the better designed retirement villages, I believe, needed to be seen in the greater community. Drive is needed to design and construct innovative passive homes and 'village' communities – healthy and highly energy efficient. And who better to call on than Professor Philippa Howden-Chapman and her experience in housing and health issues and sustainable cities. We currently experience a housing and accommodation crisis – the New Zealand marketplace proving it is unable to provide for basic accommodation needs. It has significant shortcomings in its ability to provide a sense of community. It continues to drive the cancerous sprawl onto the best horticultural and agricultural lands in the world.

It is possible to take all these matters into our own hands with one powerful action. Become another Singapore whereby all residential developments are publicly governed, developed and constrained within existing residential zones. And the moment is now as we fund our way out of post-Covid-19 impact and into a transformed economy. In honour of little Emma-Lita Bourne, let's build public housing that doesn't kill children. And what of the notion to specify the number and type of homes to be allocated within a given property development, pre-sell those allocations, and enable those purchasers to help plan and design the layout for it. A community built for and by those who would live there. Communities would start to form even before buildings are built and people have moved in. Let's build vibrant, living communities and treat the streets as extensions of our living rooms and backyards – places where teenagers and the elderly can hang-out and enjoy the company of friends *and you, too.*

Nurturing Nature

Today there is general consensus we have over-reached on dairying productivity. But that was preceded by both government agency and agricultural industry reticence to acknowledge critical issues as public consternation grew stronger about increasing greenhouse gas emissions and adverse impact on water use and water quality.

Industrial farming, big irrigation, and water quality and quantity have become issues bigger than which local authorities can be expected to cope – demonstratively illustrated by two significant events in the last decade. First, the Kaipara District Council's inability, 2012, to project manage and finance the Mangawhai waste-water treatment plant. Second, (preceded by the 2012 outbreak in the Canterbury town of Darfield) the campylobacter outbreak in Havelock North 2016, that resulted in the largest outbreak of waterborne disease in the developed world. In economists' lingo, the Havelock North event was a classic example whereby the benefits of activities are privatised and the costs of externalities are socialised. Those benefitting from agricultural pollution – farmers and their investors – are displacing the costs of pollution on to the public, requiring ratepayers to pay for deeper wells or the installation of chlorine or UV treatment plants. These matters raise the fraught issue in public debate whether or not to introduce water taxes as a means to better manage and cover costs of river and lake pollution, and drinking water contamination.

After a decade of governance that turned a blind eye to these matters, there is now desire to put hands on deck to do something about them. The good news is farm management practices exist right now that can lower stocking rates, reduce nitrogen inputs, remove stock from wet-winter soil as well as reduce gas emissions by 15 percent. Armed with this information, the Ardern-Robertson administration is on a mission to reduce cow numbers, clean up our waterways, wetlands and estuaries and improve water quality. It established WaterNZ to centralise water security and drinking water standards. And given many local authorities are unable to adequately resource water quality infrastructure and management, or restore the ecological health of our lakes, rivers and streams, July 2020 the Government announced Covid-19 recovery stimulus packages of hundreds of millions of dollars to kick-start the upgrade of drinking, waste- and storm-water infrastructure – and natural freshwater restoration projects. Largely driven by Green Party members of Parliament, freshwater restoration will be expensive and piecemeal, and open to challenge in that it treats the symptoms of pollution as opposed to the root causes of land management practice. Nevertheless, the projects are indicative of a long-awaited shift in attitude that acknowledge long-time problems.

The endangerment of wildlife, arising from our history of landscape denudation, is exacerbated by introduced pest mammal species. In 2017 the Key-English Government got on board with the independent trust Predator Free New Zealand, founded and chaired by Sir Rob Fenwick in 2013, which supports volunteers and community conservation groups dedicated to killing rats, stoats, weasels, ferrets, possums and wild cats. That administration joined in to administer funding and target the very ambitious goal to be predator free by 2050. Being the cynic I am, it seemed rather convenient to support volunteer action while increasingly emasculating the Department of Conservation with ever-tightening budget constraints. That fact, too, was not lost on the out-going Parliamentary Commissioner for the Environment, Jan Wright, in her May 2017 report on endangered wildlife and a budget-constrained Department of Conservation.

Worse for wear we are arguably a little bit wiser. Nothing short of heroic efforts have been undertaken by New Zealanders – volunteers and government agencies alike – to help support viable populations of endangered species. Conservationist Don Merton, and his work within our previous day NZ Wildlife Service, provides history and context to such efforts and is worthy of special mention. Merton is renowned for bringing the Chatham Island black robin back from the brink of extinction by a fostering programme which involved the robins being incubated by Chatham Island tomtits. The robin, once reduced to one ageing female in a population of five birds, is now survived by a population of two to three hundred. He pioneered offshore island rescue programmes where offshore islands are systematically cleared of introduced pest species, and endangered populations of indigenous wildlife are resettled to live life unpestered – continued today by the Department of Conservation.

Too, there are 'ecological islands' on the mainland – sanctuaries for wildlife protected by predator-proof fencing. *Zealandia* in Wellington is renowned – a 225-hectare restored natural area responsible for the greatly increased number of bird sightings in Wellington suburbs, not just of tūī and kererū but kāka, hihi (stitch bird), tīeke (saddleback). Tīeke was declared extinct on the mainland in 1910. Today they are breaking out over the security fence of *Zealandia* into urban Wellington. *Zealandia* has inspired other mainland ecological island projects such as the 7.7-hectare lowland podocarp forest remnant of Riccarton bush in Christchurch, and the largest such project near Cambridge, the Maungatautari Restoration, enclosing 3500 hectares of the Waikato mountain.

Japan and England are island states of similar size to New Zealand but have much greater populations of people, and histories of landscape management quite different from that of ours. The Japanese, with a population 126 million plus, twenty-eight times that of New Zealand, live in highly concentrated urban centres while they retain 68 percent of their rural landscape in non-productive forest cover. And anyone who has visited countryside England, with a population 65 million plus, fourteen times that of New Zealand, has enjoyed picturesque agriculturally productive landscape in a way that ours is not. Waterways are treed, fields are partitioned by hedgerows some containing substantial trees, and woodlots are to be seen on hillsides and hilltops, enabling viable native wildlife populations. Admittedly, English agriculture is nowhere near as efficient as that of New Zealand but we could learn something here. New Zealand's agricultural landscapes – founded on the principle that every tree trunk and every ponded wet area was wasted grass-growing space – are monochromatic and barren, cordoned off with rank growth, denuded of New Zealand character and identity. After decades of public conversation and industry tardiness, the fencing-off of livestock from our waterways on agriculturally productive lands is now taken seriously. Not for the issue of wildlife management but for that of degraded water quality in our rural landscapes. Revegetation of riparian lands is the necessary next step for wildlife management purposes.

Our traditional approach to land husbandry has been to allocate land as either highly protected or highly productive, and neither the twain to meet. For the 150 years that pastoral farming has been the economic backbone of the country, the industry model has been to focus on land conversion and increasing stock intensity. We now face the reality that this approach has reached its economic, social and environmental limits. The opportunity to make great on this challenge and move toward more multi-functional landscapes is being thrust upon us. If one is to believe the hype, a revolution in synthetic proteins is upon us.

The momentum and transition toward synthetic animal-food is underpinned by a strong moral impetus – the need to confront the dire environmental issues of global biodiversity loss and climate change. The portent could be a disjointed backbone for a small nation dependent on a pastoral farming economy. New Zealand's short and recent history is a classic case study of a historical global trend seen in microcosm – that of human beings so heavily dominating the landscape, indigenous plants and animals are pushed into oblivion. Industrial pastoral agriculture is not only hugely consuming of land and water and a major contributor to water pollution, but also a major contributor to greenhouse gases – both issues we currently grapple with. Top that off with the high cost of health issues in developed nation economies associated with high meat diets and low consumption of vegetable, grains and pulses. A shift to a synthetic protein, plant-rich diet ticks all the boxes with regard to promotion of human health and earth health.

Yet, nothing is ever so straight forward – always the devil in the detail. In the New Zealand context, thanks to Maui's brothers, much of our lands are not suitable for other food production – our topography lends itself to hillside grazing and production of meat, wool and leather. In contrast, soybeans require vast areas of flat land. And let's not forget that New Zealand's pastoral red-meat production is among the most emissions-efficient in the world. And there is yet room for improvement.

Our nation's vulnerabilities have been highlighted by Covid-19 impact. It is opportunistic and timely to re-envision a decarbonised and resilient economy. With regard to nature and agriculture, opportune to normalise *regenerative* food production practices with focus on artisan and organic produce – preferably in combination. Not just in dairy but vegetables, fruit and berries – a cue to be taken perhaps from our wine, craft-beer and honey industries. Beekeeping has always been one of those industries that transgresses the boundaries of our traditional approach to land husbandry of either highly protected or highly productive landscape. If interested in reverting land from pasture and forestry to native vegetation, mānuka can provide an excellent primary coloniser with an associated income stream. Maybe this is one of those opportunities to maintain land in smaller scale farming, off which artisan and organic foodstuff is produced off land bearing indigenous vegetation, recreating animal wildlife habitat. I know it sounds all rather *Shangri-la* but the colours evoked are richer than the monochrome with which we live. And does not beekeeping allow for small owner–operators, while the bigger players market the product, Fonterra-business-style?

It was legendary conservationist Don Merton who described our flora and fauna as our national monuments. We cannot boast built heritage the likes of Europe but our natural 'architecture' is outstanding, predating anywhere else on Earth by tens of millions of years. No one else has our kauri, podocarp or tree ferns. No one else has kiwi, kakapo or tuatara. This is our natural architecture to which our national identity is linked. With time it is to be hoped we can re-establish distinctive New Zealand natural character in our productive landscapes as we mature economically and socially.

Botanist and author Philip Simpson has a similar philosophy to his line of work as my dentist to his. My dentist's is *look after your gums and your teeth will look after themselves*. Simpson's is *look after the processes of life and the individuals will look after themselves* – the individuals being trees. Simpson has written books on signatory Aotearoa/New Zealand trees representing nationhood and our unique natural environment – pōhutukawa and rata, totara, and tī kōuka (cabbage trees). He explores their legendary origins, cultural values for both Māori and Pākehā (practical and artistry), and matters of politics and conservation. Simpson states, 'I try to see plants as the latest version of their genealogy, or whakapapa, and I try to regard individuals or species not as things but as processes'[2]. He is of the view we can take the concept of *mauri* (life force) and apply it to strengthen Pākehā interests in restoring ecological health to the land.

David Crutchley is the farmer/proprietor of Shortlands Station, a family-owned high country station in Maniototo, Otago. While he may smirk at the notion of restoring the flow of *mauri* within environment, he is doing just that. And he is making money from a reputable business to boot. His high-quality meat is marketed under the trading name, Provenance. He wished to leave a legacy of a viable farming business to his family. Despite doing the 'right' things over the years as advised to irrigate and apply more and more agrichemicals, his farm was producing less and less. The land was dead. Its history of industrial farming had depleted soil quality, animal health and farm productivity. Today he is a success story for a newly coined term – *regenerative farming*. It took him ten years to recreate 'living soil' with mixed pastures of grasses and herbs, and minimal use of fertilisers. His meat product, sought and sold internationally and to select domestic clientele, is hormone and antibiotic free with no artificial ingredients or colouring.

The biodiversity of Aotearoa/New Zealand is a heartfelt aspect of our culture, identity and well-being. Indeed, landscape is an embedded component within our national psyche. Yet the trend in land conversion to pasture, plantation forestry, suburbs and lifestyle blocks continues to reduce the extent of our native land cover, coastal lowland wetlands and sand dunes. We have imagined ourselves as predator free by 2050. The Labour coalition Government envisaged

New Zealand to be carbon neutral by 2050. Is it too far-fetched to be inspired by the successes and philosophies of Zealandia Wildlife Sanctuary, David Crutchley of Provenance meats, Philip Simpson's focus on nature's whakapapa, and the notion of a 'Fonterra-style honey marketer'? Can we imagine a post-Covid-19 reset of magnificence – New Zealand as a producer and global supplier of quality artisan and organic foodstuffs, produced in a landscape that does not *need* to have national parks?

Constitutional Relief

Debate over the need or otherwise for a constitution, swings between strictures by which government can be held to account, or loose arrangements that evolve with the changing values of society. Those who argue the latter are of the view our current day package of key pieces of legislation, legal documents, court decisions and conventions that cover constitutional matters is sufficient – and should not that package be free to evolve over time? As opposed to a constitution that would set in stone the assumptions, attitudes, beliefs and prejudices of a comparatively small group of people living in a particular period of time – examples of which we witness in the 'right to bear arms' written into the 18th-century American Constitution and the 100-year-old citizen status stipulation that tripped up a number of Australian politicians mid-2017, who unbeknown to themselves were eligible for dual citizenships. And why should it be the courts calling governments to account, rather than the electors in our small and intimate parliamentary democracy?

Because, argue constitutional lawyer Sir Geoffrey Palmer QC and litigator Dr Andrew Butler – who spearheaded a nationwide debate on how a New Zealand constitution could look – fundamental societal values are at risk in not being codified. They argue the current package of law and conventions are incomplete, obscure, fragmentary, too flexible and short of constraints on government and parliamentary power[3]. Our democracy comprises of Parliament (the House of Representatives) which makes law. The Government (the Executive) administers the law and runs the country. The judiciary, through the courts, interprets the law. Palmer and Butler argue that New Zealand is so exposed to the whim of majority rule that with a simple majority of 61 of the 120 members, Government can make, repeal or amend almost any law it pleases in a single sitting day of the House under urgency, without public input – including our constitutional laws such as the Constitution Act 1986 and the Bill of Rights Act 1990.

Three controversial cases were demonstrations of a government's readiness to do exactly this when it was deemed in its interests to do so. In 1997, a successful application was made to the Māori Land Court for it to determine whether the foreshore and seabed of the Marlborough Sounds was Māori customary land. The High Court overruled that Court's right to consider the matter. In 2003 the Court of Appeal ruled in favour of the Māori Land Court decision. To prevent the Māori Land Court from considering the case, the Government enacted the Foreshore and Seabed Act 2004 and deemed the title to be held by the Crown. When families caring for severely disabled adult loved ones took Government's refusal to pay for that care to the Human Rights Review Tribunal, they won their case: the case being that refusal to pay amounted to unjustifiable discrimination under the Bill of Rights Act. They successfully defended and won Government challenges in the High Court, then the Court of Appeal. The Government's follow-up response was to amend the Public Health and Disability Act under urgency on Budget night 2013 removing the initial right of appeal to the Human Rights Commission. In 2010, ostensibly due to controversy over the

Canterbury Regional Water Management Strategy (being vetoed by principled Councillors), Government sacked the entire democratically elected Canterbury Regional Council and replaced it with appointed Commissioners. With the appointment of Commissioners, controversial big agri-business irrigation schemes in the McKenzie Basin were enabled, pushing the Government's agenda for more cows. A hybrid council was established six years later in 2016 but full democratic rights were not fully restored until 2019.

With the enactment of the Constitution Act 1986, New Zealand revoked all residual United Kingdom legislative power and annulled the power of the United Kingdom Parliament to legislate for New Zealand. Since its enactment, New Zealand has stood as a free-standing constitutional monarchy whose Parliament has unlimited sovereign power. It is the unlimited sovereign power and the ability to strip the basic rights of citizens, as in the examples above, that is of concern to many. And it was, indeed, the motivation when Geoffrey Palmer, then Minister of Justice in the Lange Labour Government, crafted the Bill of Rights Act 1990 – which includes the Treaty of Waitangi. Sir Geoffrey has long advocated the need for a New Zealand constitution and in this instance he wished the Bill of Rights Act to become supreme law and thus the Treaty to become supreme law – causing some erosion of Parliamentary sovereignty in that it would have required a 75 percent majority vote in the House of Representatives to amend or repeal. Select Committee review decided New Zealand was not ready for a Bill of Rights in this form and recommended it be introduced as an ordinary statute.

New Zealand as of yet, has never had a deep conversation about its constitutional arrangements. Early 2018, Sir Geoffrey and Dr Butler published their book *Towards Democratic Renewal* – the result of follow-up nationwide consultation on their earlier 2016 book *A Constitution for Aotearoa/New Zealand*. Amongst other things, Sir

Geoffrey and Dr Butler suggest a crackdown on legislative urgency so that draft law cannot be rushed through Parliament without due process and proper consultation; greater transparency by requiring full explanation of legislative proposals; a four-year Parliamentary term so that governments have time to more properly consider legislation; making the Parliamentary Speaker politically independent; and requiring decisions about international relations (such as trade partnerships), defence, and commitment to go to war, to be made by Parliament (not Government).

Important, too, is the defining of our bicultural, socially liberal society and to ensure New Zealand's essentially tolerant social consensus endures. New Zealand has moved on from the Pākehā dominated culture pre-1980s and become a multi-racial nation. Given our diverse ethnic make-up, and the increasing influx of Middle Eastern, African and Asian migrants, there is arguable need to enshrine and make explicit the rules and principles that govern us and by which New Zealanders live and value. Today a quarter of our population, over a million New Zealanders who share the country, were not born in New Zealand, and these peoples bring with them values and beliefs not always in keeping with the history and the core values that underpin New Zealand's political and social traditions. For example: the role of Māori as tangata whenua; freedom of thought, conscience and religion; the importance of the place of women in society; our liberal abortion laws; the rights of workers and children; and freedom of sexual orientation. The quid pro quo will be protection of the rights of ethnic, religious and linguistic minority groups to enjoy their culture, use their language and profess and practice their religion.

Sir Geoffrey and Dr Butler have not been the only people beavering away on such a heavy issue as constitutional reform. The previous Key-English National Government and its Māori Party coalition partner pursued independent but complementary work efforts of their own. And so it should be. These matters are of such import the broadest spectrum of perspective is a must. That government's Constitutional Review Panel report recommended setting up a process to explore in more detail the idea to add economic, social, cultural and environmental rights to the NZ Bill of Rights Act. Examples of which could include rights to housing and education, which cannot be enforced directly by the courts. And of current day topic, why not safe, clean waste, storm and drinking waters? Too, should not decisions about communication security matters (read our participation in the Five Eyes spy network) be a decision made by Parliament (not Government)?

Sir Geoffrey and Dr Butler came away from their nationwide conversations persuaded that New Zealand was in need of democratic renewal – hence their revised book's namesake. There is proposal for a Head of State to be known as a kaitiaki with some powers to protect the constitution, including New Zealanders' basic rights and liberties. They acknowledge that the proposal for constitutional protection of the Treaty of Waitangi requires further conversation to establish common ground on what the Treaty means. Yet, there is unresolved debate about whether the Treaty should be included – inclusion being opposed by many Māori who fear it will become prescriptive in nature – losing its 'living document' status open to interpretation.

Any proposed constitution would need to articulate the status and relationship with the Treaty of Waitangi. There are cans of worms to be found when crunching Treaty issues. Bill English hit the nail on the head of one such can, when addressing dignitaries at Orākei Marae[4]. With upcoming elections on the horizon, Bill English was endeavouring to align Māori sentiments with those shared by the National Party – that of self-reliance and a natural scepticism of the State. The *can* is that of tino rangatiratanga. It's a test, regularly, noted English. 'If you keep following the path beyond Māori scepticism of the State, you end up with having to define tino rangatiratanga and trying to reconcile partnership with a unitary state. There is a natural tension between the Māori view of partnership and their traditional models of leadership, and the democratic process. We [government] get to reassert the primacy of the democratic process, which is fundamentally democratic, not fundamentally about partnership. The partnership can only go so far. Being able to draw the line is a critical part of the relationship.' Further conversation to establish common ground on what the Treaty means before being entrenched within a constitution, would need to do just that – define the reach of partnership and *draw the line.*

New Zealand is blessed with unique socio-political circumstances and we need to consider how we differ from others, and how those differences might be encapsulated in constitutional form.

In endeavour to define the reach of partnership and *draw the line,* could not New Zealand think beyond the UK's standard Westminster model of the traditional tripartite separation (the_Executive, legislature and judiciary)? Could not Māori iwi be a fourth part of government?

These matters were addressed by the 2015 Matike Mai Aotearoa report assisted to completion by lawyer, academic and campaigner Moana Jackson[5]. The report is the product of the Independent Working Group on Constitutional Transformation. It was a Māori-led project – convened at the same time the government of the day launched its Constitutional Review Panel. The Matike Mai Aotearoa report offers several models that propose an assembly of iwi and hapū alongside Parliament. It is suggested that such an assembly could reflect Article Two with its protection of tino rangatiratanga, with Parliament reflecting Article One with reference to kāwanatanga (governance), and a further 'relational sphere' allowing interaction between the two.

These matters, too, were addressed by Max Harris in *The New Zealand Project*. He raises the notion of a constitutional model that includes an elected Executive to fulfil Treaty obligations, alongside a more diverse legislative assembly to hold the Executive to account.

Such thinking is in keeping with recognition that separate arrangements for Māori are not so much racism, but their legal right. Whatever the form or shape of a New Zealand constitution, the argument for one is it would establish clarity, certainty and accessibility, and if judges were given the power to invalidate legislation inconsistent with the constitution, it would help to prevent abuses of political power.

Governing Governance

The closest I have come to national politics was my acquaintance when in the employ of the Commission and then the Ministry for the Environment. It was time enough for me to realise that every person who involved themselves in New Zealand politics did so for altruistic reasons. While recent year politics have challenged that insight, in the main, most want to contribute and make a difference – to help shape and move New Zealand into a place they consider to be an improved state. Even if I don't agree with what that is. Too, came the realisation that the debating chamber was little more than a stress-release forum. The grunt and detailed work efforts and decision-making are undertaken in select committee procedures prior to the matters being formerly mooted in the chamber.

I can't help but feel our adversarial, becoming personality-driven style of politics is wasteful, inefficient, frequently just plain embarrassing, adding little to genuine democracy. Every three years we place our mark to favour a parliamentarian and a political party. Then again we are subject to another three years of puerile public posturing and banter between political cliques that privately drink together in the same bar.

In a lowly populated, small nation, do we really need multiple party politics? New Zealand party politics has its roots in tensions between the interests of the farming fraternity and the mining and waterfront industries, laying the foundations for the two main National and Labour parties that largely dominated New Zealand political history. Today blue- and white-collar employment has become blurred. And we are in a time when the importance of class-based politics has been diluted by our MMP system of multi-party representation – where coalition formation depends on how the parties and compromises line up around the political issues of the day.

I like the picture of Nelson settler farmers, the Holyoake and Rowling families, who were neighbours for more than a hundred years. Apparently, neighbourly interactions entailed many a vigorous political debate and both families produced New Zealand Prime Ministers – albeit, sitting on opposing parliamentary benches. I cite this anecdote because, by and large, we are a nation of three million eligible voters of single ideology and to some extent the two main parties are mirror reflections of family members – maybe cousins, different but closely related. Regardless of personal bent and party persuasion, politicians and their parties have to tread as close to middle-of-the-road as their compromises permit, to gain the support required to string together a majority or coalition in the house.

Rather than allowing policies to be vote-catchers owned by a particular party, should they not represent Parliament and the best interests of the nation? In this day and age, it is not about being *left* or *right*, it's about being forward-looking and progressive. Could we not save ourselves the bother in costs of time, money and bureaucracy and be done with the farce of multi-party politics in New Zealand?

While we have multi-party politics, I am an advocate for our MMP system. But I now go out on a limb and speak the unspeakable: *the benefit of having no credibility to lose*. Could we function as a non-party state? And in so doing, side-step celebrity politics, commodification and the non-constructive bickering designed simply to appeal to a fragile voting base. What if we return to the simplicity of a first-past-the-post voting system to vote for those we think best fit to represent our electorates. Send them to the chambers of the Beehive, let them partake in robust debate and be at liberty to be counted in accord with their conscience, and the views of their electorates, free of the constraints of party creed and politicking.

It was how central government functioned from the mid-1850s until the turn of the century when party politics began to evolve. Perhaps it is telling that we found the model inadequate and party representation evolved to meet political needs. And telling that the model has been operative in local government for 150 years and few people have interest in local government politics. But I persevere. In the day, the General Assembly was structured as a bicameral Parliament consisting of a Governor, a Legislative Council (the upper house) a House of Representatives (the lower house), and six Provincial Councils. The upper house was in place for 100 years before being abolished in 1950. And current day thinking on constitutional reform has raised the notion of several different models comprising different houses, and assemblies of iwi and hapū alongside Parliament.

We have well-established and operational regional governments in place. Is it too far-fetched that candidates voted in on a first-past-the-post basis, making decisions in a bicameral Parliament alongside a

Māori assembly, could function in conjunction with regional councils that are required to operate strongly deliberative democratic practice. Would this be a cheaper system to operate and administer and would it incur wider public participation and interest in both central and regional politics?

Of course, any such notions would have to be debated within the frame of a written constitution. What checks would we need on the Executive? Would we vest more authority on the judiciary and/or choose to become a republic, and in turn, what type of republic? With an upper and lower house is there need for a president? Would we choose to have a president with veto powers, some powers, or no more power than the Governor-General?

The question whether to become a republic or remain a democratic constitutional monarchy may be a quandary for us. Notwithstanding a role similar to that of a Governor-General, being a president would require swagger not in keeping with how we go about our daily affairs – power invested in a single personality is not the Kiwi way. I like Simon Bridges' expression of discomfort: 'A democratically elected president would entail a Helen Clark or a John Key coming back . . . I'm a reluctant monarchist',[6] paraphrasing Winston Churchill's thought on capitalism in that *it's the worst possible system except for all the others*. Bridges is opposed to the idea of appointing people on the basis of heredity, but accepts that constitutional monarchy works for us. All in keeping with the theory of collective myth making. He states, 'Neither the Queen nor the Governor-General has any actual power, nor the means to acquire any, and it's a cheaper, lower-key office to maintain than that of a president . . .' As a footnote, Sir Michael Cullen adds that 'if you look around the world, those countries that have symbolic monarchies do rather better than those that don't in terms of human rights'[7].

Community of Commonwealth

At one time our social and political alignments were unalienable – assumed and unquestioned. We were a part of the British Empire and to be otherwise was unthinkable. As our trade links and military history with Britain weakened, we began to identify more strongly with Pacific Rim nations and that included an interest in closer trade and political ties with America. Closer political and by implication military association with America has always been a somewhat fraught question for Kiwis. While there is natural commonality in our spawning from British capitalism and imperialism, we have long been wary of the arrogance of American hegemony.

I have counted myself amongst those who have considered the Commonwealth of Nations to be a historical anachronism. I am a recent convert otherwise. Jane Clifton canvassed the matter of their relevance following the most recent Commonwealth Heads of Government Meeting (CHOGM)[8]. By her account the meeting was an unprecedented charm offensive by both Britain and the royal family as they face-up to the prospect of being no longer relevant and made redundant by the fifty-two member commonwealth countries. Commonwealth nations are seeking collective trade agreements with a new ambition to form their own trading bloc. The Secretary-General Patricia Scotland, citing research and analysis by the Commonwealth Secretariat stated, 'the cost of doing business between Commonwealth countries is on average 19 percent cheaper than between non-member countries'. They are a cohort of states with inherited commonalities – *common language, common law, common institutions, common parliamentary structures*. And English language common to all members enables communication without ambiguities.

The 'club' has endured as a coherent bloc because of its collective ethos. Out of its colonial origins it has morphed into a sort of quality assurance association – its members required to uphold labour force, human-rights and environmental standards. As well as the development of professional standards the Commonwealth has spawned social, professional and educational institutions, including the Commonwealth Games and student exchanges. CHOGM provides a forum for the airing of disagreements, lessening the chance for differences ever escalating to war between member states. Tensions between India and Pakistan are pushing this paradigm to the limit. And while accounting for the pariah states of Zimbabwe and Fiji (which were expelled) and highly questionable politics in Kenya, the Commonwealth has endured as a champion and exemplar of democratic freedoms.

With a combined population of 2.4 billion, the Commonwealth bloc of countries includes a third of the world's population. That is a marketplace that includes India's 1.26 billion people, as well as the large Asian economies of Malaysia and Singapore. It includes nineteen members states in Africa, the second largest continent in the world, highly regarded as a potential growth market. Secretary-General Patricia Scotland says the bloc is on course to exceed 1.5 trillion pounds sterling in intra-member trade by end 2030. Given current day trade-war tensions between the United States and China (and more recently between Australia and China), the Commonwealth has potential to function as a bulwark against overt protectionism and a force capable of clearing capital-roadblocks for developing countries, satisfying Winston Peter's longstanding concern regarding our singular reliance on China. To increase the growth dividend, member states great and small would need equal voice. For example, when island states express concern about rising sea-levels, the bloc of Commonwealth nations can be the platform on which to stand and be heard. That sentiment is very much in keeping with Jacinda Ardern's aspiration to facilitate a collective voice with South Pacific island states.

I find the prospect of a trading bloc inclusive of a third of the world's population, with nation states that share historical commonalities, a prospect worthy of pursuit. So, too, it would seem does Britain as it eyes former colonies to plug a post-Brexit trade gap. As Britain goes through its tortuous divorce proceedings with the EU, it sees the possibility of a new game being played by its former client states. Not wanting to be left on the side-line, it, too, is keen to learn to play ball according to the new rules of any new game – willing to let go of the patronising and self-interested lens of old through which it has historically viewed its Commonwealth members. A Commonwealth free-trading bloc would require a significant overhaul of CHOGM's administration. To kick the game off requires CHOGM to get its act together, to be more focussed and proactive.

ANZUS-ZAC or NZ?

Today, a young Kiwi's OE will typically include a pilgrimage to Turkey. It has become a must-see on the OE circuit for any self-respecting backpacker to attend ANZAC Day commemoration at Gallipoli as an occasion to identify with and express New Zealand nationhood. In contrast, many of the post-war generation of baby-boomers in the 1960s–70s didn't attend ANZAC services. Because if you did, it was a political statement that you accepted the values of the Returned Serviceman's Association, which at that time included an acceptance of New Zealand's involvement supporting the Americans in the atrocity and tragedy of Vietnam.

For New Zealanders, Gallipoli is the site, beachhead and hillslope, where we attempted to invade a country with which we had no quarrel, and which resulted in disastrous consequences and massive defeat. Understandably, Gallipoli is recognised by the Turks as a formative moment in their national identity when Kemal Ataturk established his reputation, and the beginnings of modern Turkey. I can understand the sacredness of the site where so many lives were lost, and how it has become a site of commemoration jointly by both invaded and the invader. But what has it been over the past forty years in New Zealand that has given the disaster of Gallipoli its nationhood-forming status?

ANZAC Day remembrance, and the ritual of paying our genuine respects to the dead, tends to preclude any depth of reflection or atonement – reflection on the causes of war and, in the case of Gallipoli, any expressions of regret that we might have been in the wrong place at the wrong time. Our misadventure at Gallipoli was more to ingratiate ourselves to King and Empire than any notion of altruistic ideals. The Ottoman Empire was in collapse and the British thought that it might be strategically advantageous to have a piece of it. We gallantly joined forces with the motherland to support her in her opportunistic ventures with the expectation of a share of the spoils of war. As indeed was the case when German island colonies Nauru and Samoa became New Zealand colonies.

Gallipoli was an exercise in imperialism within which we participated with our parents and cousins – Britain and Australia. We are three of the cohort of five that comprise the current day Five Eyes spy network, jointly with Canada and America. The Waihopai facility in Blenheim is New Zealand's component of the surveillance network.

In 2008, teacher Adrian Leason, farmer Sam Land and Catholic priest Peter Murnane entered the Waihopai spy base in Blenheim and disabled a satellite-signal interceptor – one of two very large, inflated, white, covered puffball-like dome structures. The three, charged with criminal damage and burglary, were acquitted by the District Court on the basis that they were driven by a belief that the spy base caused human suffering. In the High Court, 2010, the Crown successfully sought $1.2 million in a civil case. In 2013, the Court of Appeal heard the three's appeal and ruled in favour of the High Court, supporting the Crown. With all the odds against them the three appealed further to the Supreme Court.

Then the Government let the case drop – the reason given, it was a hopeless case – the accused were financially challenged. Having reached the level of the Supreme Court the Government's rationale lacked credibility. Perhaps the more likely reason was Government's concern for potential damage the publicity could have done if the Supreme Court allowed the three to argue their case. It was 2014 – election year, and the Key-English Government had had a discomforting 2013 with the Dotcom fiasco and countering accusations of spying on New Zealand citizens.

Instead of sending a policeman to knock on Kim Dotcom's door, the Government supported a stupendously stupid Hollywood-style helicopter SAS commando raid on his home to charge him with US copyright infringements (a civil case in New Zealand). Subsequently, Dotcom accused the Government of cooperating with the US National Security Agency (NSA) and of using the Government Communications Security Bureau (GCSB) to spy on him. February 2020, he lost his bid for damages against the GSCB and he awaits a separate decision on whether he can be extradited to the US for copyright-related charges

In 2013, the Government amended the GCSB Act to extend its ability to collect significant amounts of data about New Zealanders' communications. Despite warnings from the New Zealand Law Society that the Bill was fundamentally flawed and vocal hostility from the public and opposition parties, the legislation was passed into law with a two-vote majority in August 2013. The amendment coincided with American whistle-blower Edward Snowden informing the European Parliament that NSA's foreign affairs division was actively pressuring and incentivising nations to change their laws to enable mass surveillance and contribute to a key American intelligence collection programme. Snowden specifically identified the Waihopai spy base as doing just that – hoovering up electronic communications in the South Pacific, including those of New Zealand citizens, and passing them on to NSA in the US.

That the Waihopai spy base is a component of the Five Eyes spy network and contributes to American intelligence collection is common knowledge. That the GCSB Act was amended in 2013 to extend its ability to collect significant amounts of data about New Zealanders' communications is given. And in hindsight, we can see that the very special case made for the rudely abrupt granting of Peter Thiel's New Zealand citizenship in 2011 comes deeply hued in shades of *yeah, right!* Most self-respecting New Zealanders were outraged when it came to light that the Key-English Government had granted Thiel, owner of big-data technology company Palantir, citizenship after a mere few days (five years for anyone else). He immediately purchased a 193-hectare former sheep station on the shores of Lake Wanaka. His citizenship application apparently warranted special treatment – he donated $1 million to a Christchurch earthquake fund and invested in New Zealand technology companies. Outrage was compounded by the fact that it was six years down the track before the granting of his citizenship come to public light. Why the secretiveness? Did his sudden incarnation as a fully-fledged New Zealander and under-the-radar application process have something to do with our spy agencies connections with Palantir as implied by Graham Adams[9]?

All the above suspiciously points to a Key-English administration that had a predisposition to kow-tow to US Government bidding to expand Five Eyes surveillance. Since its invasions of Afghanistan and Iraq, America faces more threats in more places than at any time since the Cold War. As a consequence, America has become paranoid and its 'home security' has spread its tentacles internationally, aided and abetted by increasingly pervasive domestic security laws in other nation states. New Zealand is inveigled within the designs of American security systems and NSA's surveillance agendas. This exact matter came to the fore in the aftermath of the Christchurch mosque massacre – our surveillance priorities having been focussed on beards and hijabs as opposed to 'red-necks'. Too, in the wake of the Christchurch mosque massacre there has been an awakened mindfulness of the danger of being sucked yet deeper into such an Orwellian world and all that that implies. Such as we witness in the current day techno-autocracy-enabled, dictatorial and fascist regime in China.

Following the Second World War, the USA became an informal empire constituted by military bases worldwide, economic pressures (bullying) and political coups. And it nurtured a recent year tendency to use assassination as foreign policy. It adopted a system where, within its Western club, it doesn't use military force. And by creating multilateral global institutions and submitting itself to the authority of these institutions, it was able to convince other countries that it would not threaten them. By building itself into and using international rules and regimes, the USA successfully established a global hegemonic order. Indeed, when the TPPA was in contention, America's rationale was primarily to contain China.

The pretence that the world must be made safe for democracy has provided the philosophical underpinning for US interventions around the globe for the seven decades post-World War II. It has been able to use the UN to promote its own agendas and employ its military power and double standards to impose their order on its peripheries of influence. When other nations haven't wanted to play ball the way the Americans wanted to play, US interventionist foreign policy came to the fore. It has actively bullied and manipulated others into serving its needs and wants, and been responsible for bloodletting in multiple regime changes and support of military dictatorships in the decades of interventions in Central and South America, South East Asia, the Middle East – as well as its dabbling in Africa. Non-client states not in its club (Russia, China, Middle Eastern and South American nations such as Iran and Venezuela), seeing through the façade and hypocrisies, tired of it.

There is no better example than that of Iran. After the nationalisation of its oil industry by Prime Minister Mohammed Mossaddegh, he was ousted by a military coup, 1953, at the behest of the US and the UK in order to privatise the industry, and maintain Iran as a Cold War ally with its strategic position between the Soviet Union and the Persian Gulf. At this time the US actively fostered the development of a nuclear-armed Iran before the corrupt regime of Mohammad Reza Pahlavi was overthrown by the popular Khomeini revolution in 1979. US pique has ever since led to the needling of Iran, and vice-versa, while the US and British continue to court and arm autocratic and undemocratic Saudi Arabia with its appalling human rights record and fostering of terrorist factions – and hinder international inspection and supervision of Israeli nuclear weapons.

Whatever the Gallipoli/ANZAC-inspired nation-state forming factors are, the ANZAC spirit has been called upon in latter years to participate in the so-called 'war on terror'. We have been entreated to adjoin militarily in the Middle East with those same nations complicit in Gallipoli and the Western alliance that carved up the region into nation states and spheres of influence post-World War I. British and

American imperialistic misadventures and manipulations continue in the Middle East. We have managed in the main to keep aloof – but to become even more involved than what we are, in any one of these confusing fiascos, risks being involved in pointless Middle Eastern military follies akin to that of Gallipoli. The gore and debauchery of recent year multi-factional conflicts is now the cause of the greatest displacement of peoples in any region since the Second World War. While the West has disproportionately benefited from capitalist-militarism in the Middle East, there is no acknowledgement of responsibility for the current day state of affairs, the plight of most refugees being a direct result of the greed inherent in these misadventures.

Not a lot of the above has much to do with a treatise on New Zealand – which is exactly my point. Do we really wish to be associated with such extremes of capitalist adventurism and Western imperialism, while becoming more deeply inveigled in the reach of State surveillance?

The question sits begging, what are the benefits of our participation in the Five Eyes spy network other than to attract unwanted cyber activity spying on our affairs and disrupting our communications and data systems? It, too, challenges our connectedness with Australia and the recent year strains on a historical friendship (which it genuinely is). Our mutual colonial histories and social and economic interconnectedness are intertwined, so much so that no one has inclination or desire to unravel it. Yet our Australian cousins have developed different political and ethical values to that of ours – so much so it is easy to consider Australia as America's 51st state. Malcolm Turnbull, when Prime Minister 2017, openly stated Australia was joined at the hip with America – where America goes, Australia goes. No questions asked!

Our ANZAC cousins have become as paranoid as their ANZUS treaty party *minus the NZ*. As well as going unthinkingly arm-in-arm into American military forays, perhaps arguably of more concern are recent year trends abrogating ethical principles, the likes of which would never be tolerated in New Zealand – their treatment of asylum seekers and suppression of freedom of the press being classic examples. Asylum seekers treated as illegals are 'processed' offshore in containment facilities on Manus and Nauru Islands – men, women and children imprisoned without charge, without trial. And the media forbidden from reporting on the atrocious conditions and litany of incidents and mental health issues. And now, New Zealanders working and living in Australia are treated as second-class citizens without rights to social support services. And long-time New Zealand residents with criminal histories, some with little memory of New Zealand and protégés of Australian society, are being treated as illegals, deported and police-escorted back onto New Zealand soil. Surely this is not the behaviour of a member of the family?

ANZAC is a post-World War I acronym devised when Australia and New Zealand identified with being part of the British Empire. ANZUS, a post-World War II acronym devised when we felt it necessary to have a 'heavy' by our side to make sure nobody pushed us around. They have been security frameworks based on defence alliances that have us 'pack' with some nations lined up against others. It's called tribalism. In a world of multilateralism, is tribalism the way we wish to continue? Is it not time to move beyond the illusion of security through old partners and the Five Eyes spy network? I open myself to criticism of naïvety, but rather than being seen as ANZAC or ANZUS would we not look better simply as NZ? Is it not time to rethink, beyond historical military alliances that don't serve the way we wish to operate in the 21st century?

Non-Aligned Alignment

New Zealand has one of the most globalised economies in the world, the means by which we have traditionally provided for and supported our way of life. We will always be dependent on maritime trade and multilateral relationships. We pride ourselves on our good relations with many countries founded on trade, promotion of peace, and a rules-based international order. These are the factors that underpin our prosperity and security – not redundant security and defence alignments.

It remains of question; how could we possibly achieve multilateral cooperation by being counted amongst a cohort of nations posturing militarily against others? Our 1987 law to keep out nuclear weapons was more about signalling to the world that we could make our own defence and foreign policy decisions and support peaceful ways to resolve international disputes. Military posturing is not the way of multilateralism and isn't what the world is in need of. Which begs the question, how well do these principles fit with our 2018 Strategic Defence Policy Statement? That document's message: *interoperability with our traditional partners is a strategic imperative of the Defence Force.* Such a military orientation seemingly throws us back into the arms of partners who oppose our major peace achievement – the Nuclear Weapons Ban Treaty.

Would it not be a better fit for New Zealand to align with the Non-Aligned Movement (NAM)? NAM is dedicated to representing the interests and aspirations of developing countries and counts one hundred and twenty member states and seventeen observer states, whose combined population amounts to more than half of the world's population. It was formed during the Cold War by States that wished to remain neutral and not formally align with either the United States or the Soviet Union. Membership includes the adoption of independent policy based on the coexistence of States of different political and social systems, and affiliates should not be a member of a multilateral military alliance concluded in the context of Great Power conflicts. NAM has sought to create an independent pathway in world politics that does not result in member States becoming pawns in international power struggles. In the 21st century it has been vocal against the trend in global inequity and has an additional goal to facilitate a restructuring of the international economic order. Does not NAM sound a better fit for us than another Vietnam?

A New Narrative

The 21st century is setting itself up to be one of absence of hands in a global gig-economy – while trying to maintain 24/7 consumption in a world of robotic and artificial intelligence production and servicing. Proponents of AI are selling its future as the natural evolution to enable human beings to disembark from capitalism's despoiled primary resource *commodity earth*. Capitalism never solves its contradictions – exploring the galaxy is just giving the problem room to expand.

I write for Mother Earth – a world where people desire to feel the rain on their faces and splash in the puddles. Humans are soul beings. People need to *be* – to grow and develop into fully appreciative human beings, nourishing other human beings. Can we not expect more of life than simply 'living to work' – being mere chattels and servants to serve the whims of mindless corporate monopolies? It would seem money has become a dictator straitjacketing our activities, as opposed to that of a servant enabling them. We already have technologies that with equitable distribution of the benefits of time savings could reduce hours of work across the board for everyone. In a high technically capable future society our economies will be even more capable of allowing every individual the opportunity to 'work to live' – the means to a more fully lived and enriched life. Time and leisure are prime benefits citizens have fair demand to claim – why not a four-day week with more public holidays in any one year? Is this not the whole point of civil society, to secure for its members the benefits of collective action?

In the world unfolding, there will be dire need to ensure that human dignity and respect are never crushed in neoliberalism's narrowly defined aspects of value. Despite its multiple and manifest failures, we appear to be stuck with it because we have failed to produce a narrative with which to replace it. There is a dearth of noble and effective international leaders who could attempt to explain the mess we are in and offer means by which we might escape. In contrast we witness retreat into nationalism and isolationism.

We are obsessed with growth for growth's sake. There is strong correlation between global warming and extravagant wealth and consumption – climate change fed by rampant consumerism. Debunking the population myth, George Monbiot says it best: 'It's not sex; it's money'[10]. The continued degradation of human and Earth well-being is symptomatic of the impossibility of perpetual growth. It is overtime for a mind-shift in attitude – for new economic norms. The Japanese economy has been in a state of nil growth for many years and is described as an economy in recession. Yet here is a nation of millions of people, a population twenty-seven times that of New Zealand, which enjoys a high-tech first-world standard of living, in a landscape where 68 percent is in non-productive forest cover. I don't argue it is a society we aim to emulate, but is it not an example of a high-standard, self-perpetuating, stable economy?

New Zealand remains unbelievably well placed to take advantage of renewable energy sources. Energy is the great liberator of people and renewable energy the ideal way to keep climate stable. We have a history of tip-toeing around Rio Tinto and its interests in Tiwai Point smelter, manufacturing a price sensitive vulnerable commodity on which we have thought ourselves to be dependent. Given their impending departure, I am enthused by recent excitement about what we could do with excess of Manapouri hydropower. To manufacture hydrogen for high-quality silica solar panels and/or to fuel our vehicle fleet and for export when prototype hydrogen-powered aircraft take to the air – the re-establishment of new New Zealand-based industry, using New Zealand clean technology, producing green products for low-carbon purposes, employing home-based expertise and workforce, creating wealth, and money circulating within our own economy. This is the kind of thing that binds us together – re-establishes social cohesion, shared community, sense of identity, shared destiny.

We have the most efficient agricultural system in the world. We have abundant forest and maritime resources. Yet, given the relatively short period of time that people have populated Aotearoa/New Zealand, I believe that we have yet to fit and become 'of the land' – to be immersed in a mature, rich identity of place. And I do not believe this will be achieved until we have the wherewithal to inculcate *mind* into the mindlessness of neoliberalism.

In 1970s New Zealand people challenged things. In the 21st century we are going to need more of those unpredictable, contrary people. We are currently overendowed with predictable people, led by the nose by algorithms – digital profiling, propaganda and advertising that second guesses what we want and what we think. Due to the busy-ness of our daily lives we are being massaged by artificial intelligence into commoditised unthinking economic units and political automatons. As our social and commercial lives have become increasingly conducted on-line, so have the trends of narcissism, exhibitionism, hatred and loneliness arisen from a life led in full public view in the privacy of one's room. Our interpersonal skills, our attention spans and our capacity for abstract reasoning and creativity are all being undermined and compromised, when these same skills are exactly those that we will need to manage the machines of tomorrow. It has to be said again – time to revitalise our *muchness*.

CHAPTER 7
RESET

> Life is like riding a bicycle. To keep your balance, you have to keep moving.

> — ALBERT EINSTEIN

IT IS a struggle to ride a bicycle with a flat tyre. It requires extra effort, we lose steerage and if we persist, we damage the tyre. We, as a nation of peoples, have long struggled to pedal with a flat tyre, wandered on the pathway, fallen off a few times, torn the tyre and damaged the rim. New Zealand assets are largely owned by overseas corporate interests; our economy is vulnerable depending largely on providing bulk commodities to one export market; we have lost the wherewithal to provide for our own skills needs and become dependent on immigration to supply them; we have become dependent on international students to fund our secondary and tertiary education providers. We have lost the wherewithal to safely house and accommodate our populace. We experienced slippage into dirty politics and crony capitalism. Providers expect profits to be made from incarcerating people and caring for the elderly. Our sense of balance is askew – left in tatters are our predispositions for fairness, intimacy, connectedness, social coherence, sense of well-being, shared destiny, camaraderie and trust.

Malfunction in democracy and economy since the 1980s has led to disenchantment in community. Re-enchantment will need *muchness* steps to look after our own and South Pacific interests. While nurturing the dignity of our waddling but endearing kiwi, it is timely to identify more closely with the bold panache of our rumbustious tūī. Not the brash abrasive swagger of our cousins across the ditch – rather the flash of metallic emerald green and steel-blue in vigorous flight darting through trees at high speed. In so doing, bring flamboyance into our political realm and ambitions – some noisy aerobatics, even a courageous summersault or two, but always in concert with each other. Leave behind the disconnected heart of the prior thirty-five years and engage in song. Sit on a treetop, gesticulate our heads, puff out our body feathers, distend our throats, throw out variable warbles and pour forth some wild harmony of the soul.

It is timely to repair the broken wheel – fix the puncture and reinflate the tyre – reinvest in health and education, housing and infrastructure, nature and regenerative primary production, redesign of urban areas and modes of transport. A shift to a resilient, low-carbon economy, with a refreshed empathy for the landscape that supports us and the wildlife we share it with. Opportune for a transformative and comprehensive re-envisioning of Aotearoa/New Zealand – a post-Covid-19 reset of magnificence.

We could do no better than 'walk the talk' with Golriz Ghahraman's words and *stand up and be that self-righteous little nation again*: in order to put the *New* back into *Zealand*, identify more closely with Southern Cross nation states, define our sovereignty in a constitution, grow our distinctive and morphing Māori/Pākehā identity, reassert our social democratic roots, regain our sense of Kiwi fairness. Refresher courses to improve bad driving habits are required. No more cutting blind corners or cutting them in front of oncoming traffic – clear forewarned indication at intersections. All with the intent to shift New Zealand to fit Prime Minister Jacinda Ardern's vision of *a place of kindness and well-being.*

Lessons are to be had from conservationist Don Merton, who fostered and nurtured the Chatham Island black robin, bringing it back from the brink of extinction. A cue to collectively reinvest in the nurture and well-being of people – a return to an equitable distribution of wealth and income. A cue to return to the quaint old-fashioned notion we are there for one another. Then to be delightfully surprised to witness people in full chorus breaking out to excel in the freedom and security to do what they want, to pursue fulfilling lives.

Our natural architecture, predating anywhere else on Earth by tens of millions of years, is a heartfelt aspect of our landscape, cultural identity and national psyche. It is opportune to build on our unique natural heritage and high-tech primary production capabilities to re-establish distinctive New Zealand natural character in our productive landscapes. Further our skills in the most emissions-efficient agriculture in the world, and enable re-creation of indigenous vegetation and animal wildlife habitat. Fully commit to normalise *regenerative* food production practices with focus on artisan and organic produce in dairy, meat, fruit, berries and vegetables. Grow, and supply to a globally diverse marketplace, primary produce out of a landscape that does not *need* to have national parks.

In order to curtail cancerous urban sprawl and protect the diminishing assets of the best agricultural and horticultural lands in the world, take the provision for residential development out of the hands of developers. Publicly govern and develop urban intensification and supervise the design and construction of innovative, healthy and energy-efficient homes – possibly funded by a social credit slush fund such as KiwiSaver, the private sector doing the grunt work. The moment is now, while dealing with our housing and accommodation crisis. Designed with retirement village concepts with built-in recreational and health services at one's doorstep. Too, enabling viable small business proprietors – the local butcher, grocer and candlestick maker just walking distance around the corner, minimising vehicular movement. All the while creating a sense of community – living vibrancy where the streets are extensions of our living rooms and backyards. Space and venues designed and built to enable interactive and enlivened multi-ethnic community life, facilitating a renewed sense of belonging and community that New Zealanders seem to have lost.

And local commerce, those 'street corner' businesses, would be beneficiaries of a cash flow UBI-resourced populace. And I don't believe there is an alternative – people enabled to choose how to live, develop one's talents, move in and out of the employment market with ease, and actively participate in a tolerant and caring community. Lifestyles liberated by a resurrection of time, personal autonomy, social and economic surety. A dividend to which all participants within our society are eligible – cheaper to deliver than current day provisions.

For an equitable redistribution of nation economy and wealth generation, I sit with my intuitive preference for an APTT. The broadest possible tax base at the lowest possible tax rate to capture derivatives, eliminate evasion and avoidance, minimise the costs of tax administration, and enhance stability of financial markets – coherent, simple, fair, with revitalised social and public service funding to better provide for nation health, education, development of housing and infrastructure.

For those in the workforce, a new paradigm – central government agency setting wage benchmarks for all sectors of the economy in negotiation with export sector commerce and re-enabled trade and professional unions. Disruptive union activism quietened by an employer-funded support agency guaranteeing 'job transition security' – an agency that grows a nationwide pool of ready-to-be-had skills of highly motivated employees – doing away with need to depend on immigration to source those skills. Constructs that conjointly revitalise workplace morale, work ethic and productivity, entrepreneurial spirit and social cohesion.

The way out of the rabbit hole, to this world of fresh air, common sense and *Frabjous Day*, only comes with the killing of the *Jabberwocky* of unfettered neoliberal capitalism and the rampant consumerism that feeds off biodiversity loss and climate change. This is a much bigger task than that capable of our little economy down-under in the South Pacific Ocean. But the killing cannot be done by any one actor acting alone, no matter how powerful that actor. We have to be party to the murder. What we lack in economic and political clout can be compensated by participating in multilateral agendas. Exactly what Prime Minister Ardern undertook in the aftermath of the Christchurch mosque killings, convening an international summit in Paris conjointly with French President Emmanuel Macron to muster international troops and political weight to confront the likes of Facebook, Google, YouTube and Instagram to better manage their vetting of the live-streaming of violent extremist content.

New Zealand's international multilateral credibility is our *Vorpal* sword. And how much more multilateral could New Zealand get than opting out of Five Eyes, aligning with the Non-Aligned Movement with a combined population of more than half the world's population, and trading within the Commonwealth bloc of nations that includes a third of the world's population? It's the same sword required to rein in the *bandersnatches* that run loose on home turf in need of house-training. The first two thrusts of the sword would be for the carte blanche introduction of a UBI jointly with a revised tax regime.

Deft swordsmanship is required to emphasise cooperation over corporation and revitalise a public-funded informative media. The much bigger matter of constitutional reform only needs the swordsmen to stand guard. Whether we reintroduce a bicameral system of government and reconstitute for Pākehā and Māori participation and/or whether we remain a democratic constitutional monarchy, or become a republic, are all matters that will take considerable deliberation concurring with a consensus on New Zealand identity and values.

This discourse has been my personal reflection on New Zealand identity and values. To this day I enjoy New Zealand's coastline – *who doesn't?* – at one time, a wild sea on a rocky coast. I guess the taste for surging seas is in my genes. My father sailed the ocean rollers off Cape of Good Hope and cold, heavy arctic seas, while my mother grew up on rocky coastlines of Cornwall and South Wales. In latter years, I, too, enjoy the placid waters and colours of estuarine shallows – which may be more to do with my age and entering a more reflective stage of life. I was conceived on the high seas during my parents' emigration to New Zealand, and born in Matariki, the rise of Pleiades, the beginning of the Māori New Year. In contradiction, or maybe because of, I am not a winter person. I come alive in tropical temperatures and lifestyle, as my living and travel experiences on South East Asia attest to. It is the sounds and smells of New Zealand summer that I love most. Smell of salt air, beach and pōhutukawa, clear blue skies, hot tarmac, balmy evenings, good cuisine particularly Mediterranean, complemented with fine wine, the sounds of children laughing, arguing and making up, trampolines, garden hoses, suntan lotion, a fire on the beach, tūī in the flax, listening to the radio and music, having a cold beer on the back lawn on a hot day, admiring beautiful women.

Place and home is a powerful part of identity. In keeping with my childhood experience, the sense of membership to a community is partly the identity that others confer upon us – an identity that offers security and authorises 'citizenship'. I don't have a house or a village, but I do have a home – pōhutukawa coast. There is a difference between a house and a home – a house is a box, a home is where you become yourself. And I desire to ensure that I have a home in the future, not a commodified box – a Max Harris home as opposed to that of a Peter Thiel bunker. I am desirous for New Zealand to regain its *muchness* and for Kiwis to re-establish a stronger sense of community, to rebuild a collective sense of common purpose and direction.

Capitalism has run amok globally threatening democracy, and we live in a broken country. In New Zealand, in repeat of the 1880s and 1930s, an awareness has grown that privilege and poverty has again reared its head within a nation of people who profess to be egalitarian. Capitalism needs to be civilised. To civilise it, it needs to be constrained within 21st-century social-democratic parameters.

When Jacinda Ardern came to Office 2017, she proved herself to be a game-changer for the tone of politics in New Zealand. I am hopeful this change of tone is the precursor to paving the way to the refounding of innovative, socially conscious, hands-on-governance with which Kiwis have historically identified and taken pride. The 2020 Labour Government has been given a committed mandate – the support of a broad public church giving the administration confidence it has its blessings. There is promise of future prospect for me once again to feel and take pride in how New Zealand presents herself to the world, and in the values by which we live.

he tangata he tangata he tangata

BIBLIOGRAPHY

Cooke, David, et al. (eds) (2014). *Beyond the Free Market: Rebuilding a Just Society in New Zealand*. Dunmore Publishing: Auckland.

Crouch, David (2019). *Almost Perfekt: How Sweden Works and What We Can Learn From It*. Bonnier Books: Stockholm.

Doughty, Ross (1977). *The Holyoake Years*. R. Doughty: Feilding.

Duncan, Claire. 'Making Ends Meet: a brief history of State Housing in New Zealand' in *New Zealand Memories*, Jun/Jul 2017; n.126: p.38–47.

Eldred-Grigg, Stevan (2011). *People, People, People: A Brief History of New Zealand*. David Bateman Ltd: Auckland.

Ferguson, Charles (Producer, Writer, Director) (2010). *Inside Job*, Sony Pictures Classics.

Gibbs, George (2016). *Ghosts of Gondwana*. Potton & Burton: Nelson.

Gould, Bryan (2008). *Rescuing the New Zealand Economy*. Potton & Burton: Nelson.

Greive, Duncan. 'Can the Unions Save Us?' in *North and South*; Jan 2014.

Harari, Yuval Noah (2014). *Sapiens: A Brief History of Humankind*. Harvill Secker: London.

Harris, Max (2017). *The New Zealand Project*. Bridget Williams Books: Wellington.

Hill, Richard (2004). *State Authority / Indigenous Autonomy: Crown-Maori Relations in New Zealand/Aotearoa 1900–1950*. Victoria University Press: Wellington.

Hutchings, Graham (2008). *The Swinging Sixties*. HarperCollins: New Zealand.

Johansson, Jon (2009). *The Politics of Possibility: Leadership in Changing Times*. Dunmore Publishing: Auckland.

Kelsey, Jane (2016). *The Fire Economy*. Bridget Williams Books: Wellington.

King, Michael (2003). *The Penguin History of New Zealand*. Penguin Books: Auckland.

Le Heron, Richard and Pawson, Eric (eds) (1996). *Changing Places: New Zealand in the Nineties*. Longman Paul: Auckland.

Macdonald, Finlay. 'Remembering Gallipoli' in *New Zealand Geographic*. Issue 132; Apr 2015.

McLauchlan, Gordon (1976). *The Passionless People*. Cassell: New Zealand.

McLauchlan, Gordon (2012). *The Passionless People Revisited.* David Bateman Ltd: Auckland.

Meduna, Veronika and Priestly, Rebecca (2008). Lisa Matisoo-Smith in *Atoms, Dinosaurs & DNA: 68 Great New Zealand Scientists.* Random House: Auckland.

Monbiot, George (2016). *How Did We Get Into This Mess? Politics, Equality, Nature.* Verso: London.

Morgan, Gareth and Guthrie, Susan (2011). *The Big Kahuna.* Public Interest Publishing Ltd: New Zealand.

Newman, Keith. 'Rātana Church – Te Haahi Rātana' in TeAra – the Encyclopedia of New Zealand, http://www.TeAra.govt.nz/en/ratana-church-te-haahi-ratana, 2018.

Oliver, W. H. (ed) with Williams, Bridget (1981). *The Oxford History of New Zealand.* Clarendon Press: Wellington.

Palmer, Geoffrey and Butler, Andrew (2018). *Towards Democratic Renewal.* Victoria University Press: Wellington.

Piketty, Thomas (2014). *Capital in the Twenty-First Century.* Harvard University Press: Cambridge, USA.

Radford, Tim (2012). *The Address Book: Our Place in the Scheme of Things.* HarperCollins: Australia.

Rashbrooke, Max (ed) (2013). *Inequality: A New Zealand Crisis.* Bridget Williams Books: Wellington.

Rashbrooke, Max (2015). 'No Place Like Home' in *New Zealand Geographic.* Issue 132; Apr 2015.

Rashbrooke, Max (2018). *Government for the Public Good.* Bridget Williams Books: Wellington.

Sanders, Kurt (1996). *The Way We Were*. Hodder Moa Beckett: Auckland.

Standing, Guy (2011). *The Precariat: The New Dangerous Class*. Bloomsbury Academic: London.

Staples, Alex and Simmons, Geoff (2016). 'Taxing Wealth and Property – What works? A review of wealth and property taxation around the world'. Report by Morgan Foundation: New Zealand.

Stevens, Graeme (1980). *New Zealand Adrift*. AH and AW Reed: Wellington.

'Turning Point', Der Spiegel commentary reprinted in the *Australian Financial Review*; 2 Dec 2016.

Wilkinson and Pickett (2009). *The Spirit Level: why more equal societies almost always do better*. Allen Lane: London.

Wilson, John. 'New Zealand Sovereignty: 1857, 1907, 1947 or 1987?' in *Political Science* NZ Parliamentary Library. Vol 60, Issue 2, p41–50; 1 Dec 2008.

Yska, Redmer (1993). *All Shook Up: The Flash Bodgie and the Rise of the New Zealand Teenager in the Fifties*. Penguin Books: Auckland.

NOTES

1. Yeah-Nah!

1. As ranked by the International Corruption Perceptions Index since its inception in 1995.

2. Land of Two Halves

1. www.stuff.co.nz, April 2016.

3. Anatomy of Restlessness

1. Interview with Kathryn Ryan, Radio NZ, 14 October 2020.
2. *Guardian Weekly*, 30 September 2016.
3. The Penguin History of New Zealand (p491)
4. Max Rashbrooke, 2013. Inequality: A New Zealand Crisis

4. Mad Hatter's Capitalism

1. Letter to the editor, *NZ Listener*, 8 February 2014.
2. Stockholm 1972, Nairobi 1982, Rio de Janeiro 1992, Johannesburg 2002, Rio de Janeiro 2012.
3. 'The Final Straw' in *NZ* Listener, 13–19 April 2019.
4. www.interest.co.nz/charts/economy/overseas-debt
5. www.tradingeconomics.com/new-zealand/money-supply-m3
6. www.visualcapitalist.com/all-of-the-worlds-money-in-one-visualisation-2020/
7. www.wikipedia.org/wiki/National_debt_of_China
8. Reported in the *New Zealand Herald*, 23 Jan 2018.
9. www.worldbank.org/opendata
10. Joseph Stiglitz is a Nobel Prize-winning economist (for market design theory) and former Senior Vice President and Chief Economist of the World Bank.
11. Prior to its enactment, the then New Zealand Party (1983–1987) was the only Party to argue that the economic indicators of 'employment', 'exporting

competitiveness' and the 'exchange rate' should be equally weighted with the focus on inflation management.
12. Interviewed by Kathryn Ryan, Radio NZ, 8 Oct 2020.

6. Regaining Our Muchness

1. *The Big Kahuna*, 2011.
2. Preface to Philip Simpson, 2000. Dancing Leaves: the story of New Zealand cabbage trees, ti touka
3. For further information refer www.consitutionaotearoa.org.nz
4. As reported by Adrian Malloch in 'Race is On' in *NZ Listener*, 8 July 2017.
5. The report can be viewed at www.converge.org.nz
6. 'Our Mutual Friends' in *NZ Listener*, 5 May 2018.
7. Ibid
8. Ibid.
9. 'Absurdistan Revisited' in *North and South*, May 2017.
10. The Population Myth in *How Did We Get Into This Mess?* George Monbiot, 2016, (p107)

ABOUT THE AUTHOR

Variously a mechanical fitter tradesman, resource management policy analyst, lecturer, teacher and seaman, John Morgan has had a lifelong interest in natural and social history and international current affairs. Now retired, he lives by the coast in a small North Island town.

Contact: Facebook (John Morgan Author)